For my son Alexander

Live from Your Heart and Mind

The Secret to the Simplicity of Connecting Your Heart and Mind on the Road to Happiness and Success

Catherine B. Roy

Copyright 2019 by Catherine B. Roy

All Rights Reserved

Live from Your Heart and Mind / Catherine B. Roy – 2nd ed.

The information contained in this book is intended to be educational and not for any treatment whatsoever. This information should not replace consultation with a competent professional, if needed. The author is in no way liable for any misuse of the material.

No part of this publication may be reproduced, except in the case of quotation for articles, reviews, or stored in any retrieval system, or transmitted in any form or by any means, electronic, mechanical, photocopying, recording or otherwise, without written permission from the publisher. For information regarding permission, contact:

LHM International

www.catherinebroy.com

Printed in the USA

Live from Your Heart and Mind

DEDICATED TO:

For those of you who will recognize the truth of my story as your own. For those of you who are in my heart, for my family, for my friends. For those of you who will become my friends. For those of you close to me. For those of you who are far away. For you, divine people who would like to reach highest potential in life. For love, happiness and fulfillment of dreams, for peace and life...

TABLE OF CONTENTS

ACKNOWLEDGEMENTS 9

FOREWORD 11

INTRODUCTION 13

CHAPTER 1 - BALANCE 15

CHAPTER 2 - HAPPINESS 41

CHAPTER 3 - BELIEF 65

CHAPTER 4 - OBSTACLES 81

CHAPTER 5 - LOVE 97

CHAPTER 6 - SADNESS 117

CHAPTER 7 - FRIENDSHIP 133

CHAPTER 8 - VALUE 151

CHAPTER 9 - WORDS AND THOUGHTS 163

CHAPTER 10 - PEACEFULNESS 177

CHAPTER 11 - AWAKENING 189

IQ TRAINING SOLUTIONS 195

THANK YOU 205

ABOUT THE AUTHOR 211

ACKNOWLEDGEMENTS

"The more genuine gratitude you feel toward the Universe for everything you receive, the closer your relationship becomes with the Universe and that is when you can reach the level of unlimited... You will have opened your heart and mind completely to the magic of gratitude, and with it you will touch the lives of everyone you come into contact with. You will become a channel for unlimited blessings on Earth... and there will be nothing that you cannot be..."

~ Rhonda Byrne

Thank you, my reader, for giving me your time. Please try the Live from Your Heart and Mind (LHM) formulas and algorithms which were created for you in order to make your life extraordinary in every possible way! I hope this book will show you at least some other possibilities and ways of thinking that can bring you only good. I hope you will enjoy!

I wish to give a special thanks to people who helped me with this book: Patrick P. Stafford for his professional book editing services; Daryl Clark for being a great LHM webmaster, admin and content editor; Ronald Proulx for being a wonderful LHM Facebook admin who shares LHM's love and happiness with hundreds of people all over the world; Jelena Dmitrovic Manojlovic for her amazing LHM algorithms design; Majda Balic for her professional photography services and Milos Simonovic for his beautiful LHM logo design. Thank you as well to all the fabulous people who have supported LHM from the first day it was created. Thank you so much! LHM would not exist as it is if it weren't for you!

I would like to thank people who brought me positive energy, who inspired me, who gave me life lessons and who made a unique trace in my heart. Some of them I know in person. Some of them I know by their work, which found a way to me and changed me in every possible way. Even in ways I hadn't dreamed of. About all of them you will read at the end of this book.

Also, I would like to thank all the people who you will recognize in quotations at the beginning of every chapter. Many of them are no longer with us, but those are people who gave me a strong foundation for my way of understanding the most important fields in life.

Thank you.

With Love,

Catherine B. Roy

FOREWORD

Catherine and I met a few years ago and right from the start I felt that special energy in her that is required from any leader that has come to shine their light and influence in positive ways the entire world.

It is a great privilege to be a witness of all the great work Catherine continues to offer to those who are ready to transform their lives not only through the knowledge of their minds but also through what I have come to describe as the very powerful practice of heartfulness. What I found throughout this amazing life journey with all the expected and unexpected thrilling moments I have experienced so far; is that a mind without a heart cannot go as far as many believe. This is why this book is so important for you. Catherine is one of the few young leaders out there who is fully aware of the essential role of the heart when it comes to achieving the highest levels of happiness and success possible.

I could use this space to write about what you will find in the following pages but that could ruin your whole experience. I will say this though: This is a book that can change your life!

As I read one by one the pages of this book, I was able to feel the love behind the words, the feelings behind the thoughts, and the heart behind the mind that created it. It is my wish that you take full advantage of all the innovative, effective yet entertaining keys and formulas Catherine shares here with you. There has never been a better time and greater opportunity than right now to become a creative force in this world and achieve true success and happiness in your life. Use this book as a reliable guide that will enrich your life in all ways. Turn the page. Begin using your mind and your heart to create only the best. The world counts on YOU…

Roxana Jones,

Bestselling, Multi-Award Winning Author

and Spiritual Healer

http://roxanajones.com/

INTRODUCTION

What is the secret to the simplicity of *"connecting your heart and mind"* in the *road to happiness and success*? In my book here, you will find that the secret is truly simple. For the power to grasp it and know it is right in front of our eyes!

You have *read a lot of self-development books*, but *something is not working*, right? *You are not satisfied* or *you are not achieving what you expected*? Or maybe you are new to this field? Well, look no further! For now you can find out the easiest way to satisfaction and success, and both at the same time!

With proven *Live from Your Heart and Mind (LHM)* exercises, techniques and a lot of examples in this book, you can discover and accomplish the "connection between your heart and mind" so that you will be among the rare who *hit the center of the target* and are *successful and emotionally satisfied* at the same time.

As you can see, some parts of the text are illustrated for you. According to Ranko Rajovic, PhD and member of the Mensa International Committee for Gifted Children, it is scientifically proven that the human brain remembers pictures easier than text. In this case it is even more powerful because the illustrations here are directly associated with phrases and concepts expressed in this book. So allow yourself to "read" from these pictures. It will be fun, yes? But more valuable than fun is connecting and obtaining superior results in business and academia and doing better on educational tests like PISA. This has been shown to be true in Asian nations whose alphabet consists of pictorial images and symbols rather than mere linguistic letters. And it is proven that PISA test results are proportionally connected the academic growth and GDP of said nations. China is a good case in point, as it is one of the most successful on PISA tests and also one of the most successful economies in the world. Think about that!

So, in order to make it easier for you to remember, some parts of this book (marked as *text*) will be illustrated. These will be helpful associations for you, or even better, you can make your own word-phrase-concept associations. You will have fun. You will train utilizing one of the most powerful memory techniques in existence, and you will remember important parts that you will use later on in your personal life as well as in your career.

So, have fun! Enjoy! Learn! Be happy! And achieve success!

CHAPTER 1

BALANCE

"The best and safest thing is to keep a balance in your life, acknowledge the great powers around us and in us. If you can do that, and live that way, you are really a wise man."

~ Euripides

Welcome to our plane of satisfaction and success. I wish you a comfortable flight. This plane has no turbulence, it is balanced and calm. Just relax and enjoy discovering your brilliant future. We will talk about the emotional and mental balance as a prerequisite for achieving our goals and reaching the level of inner satisfaction and outer success. Very soon you will recognize the importance of the time that you now spend with me and you will see that you can be more successful than you have ever been and at the same time emotionally satisfied and fulfilled! You will learn how to practice being extraordinary so that extraordinary become your life style!

After this part of the book, we will analyze some of the most important fields in life. Then step by step you will change your frequency of life and start living the best way – the way that all of us deserve!

What I particularly want to emphasize at the beginning is:

We are the consequence of our past and at the same time the cause of our future.

This means that right now we are creating our future with every thought and with our every action. Let's see how.

We all accomplish goals in our personal life, in school and on job. So I have a question for you: "Whose goals?" Are these really our goals or are they imposed upon us? For how do you explain that *2% of the population has nearly 90%*

of the wealth in the world? This is a well-known fact, of course. So another question comes to mind: are you among them?

Well then, now when we have come to realize this, I just have to say: *Set your own goals and act to accomplish them or someone else will hire you to accomplish theirs! Be the part of the 2%!*

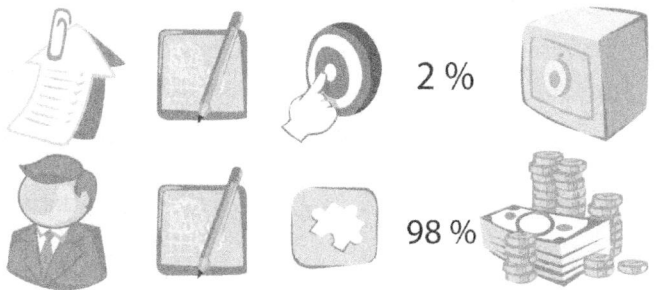

It doesn't matter where we are coming from. The only thing that matters is where are we going? Do you know where you are going? Do you really, exactly know your way?

Decision is just the first step, but actions are every step after that first one.

Do you know the story about the three frogs that are standing beside a lake and then one frog decides to jump? How many frogs are now beside the lake?

Three. For one frog decided to jump, but it didn't jump!

You can learn verified practical techniques for your own mind or emotional development and to further your intellectual skills, management tools, problem solving, etc. The Internet is full of instructors and instructions. Books about self-development are all around us. But why do many of them not work?

Because the most important thing is missing:

Until it is explicitly clear where exactly we should apply these techniques, upon our own goals or the goals of our boss, spouse, children, and what is imposed upon our own, how can we know we are on the right track?

So, if you ask yourself why you are not satisfied? First answer this: Have you set your own goals? And if you did, what are you doing to accomplish them? Because, it is not just a place where success lives, it is also a place where satisfaction lives! Do you want to be successful and satisfied? If you do, then follow me here, please.

First thing that you must do is to set your goals. I will explain to you one of the methods for setting goals later on, but now it is much more important to recognize that you are going to set the right ones. Because if you set some goals, no matter how well you do it, it is not the right way if the goals are wrong. Am I right? So prepare yourself, because now you will do one of the most important things in your life: identify that you have set the right goals.

My first question for you is: ***"How are you?"***

 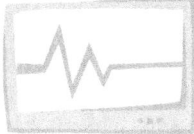

And now, maybe you think: "Is this a joke?" No, it is serious and very important. So stay focused with me, please. I do not expect an answer: "I am fine. Thanks for asking. How are you?" So I must ask you: "When was the last time you stopped for five minutes, be alone with yourself and ask: "How are you?" Have you ever? In this fast-paced world, it is very difficult to do, but you will see that it is necessary! I wonder how you really are? And with this question you will need to go inside your own soul to answer. Therefore, open the door of the inner You, and enter a world that has always existed in you, and in which are the answers to ALL your questions dwell. Trust yourself! Nobody does it better than you do. No one knows what is best for you. Neither I or your parents or spouse or friends or children or colleagues. Only the one and only you!

Now, I invite you to do a very important, nice breathing exercise. Choose some pleasant, calm music, music that you like, or do this exercise in complete silence. My recommendation is music from the film "The Secret." You can find it on YouTube by the name The Secret to You...A Gift from The Secret Scrolls. If you do choose this video, please don't watch it. We will do that together later on.

Now, just play the music. Close your eyes, and begin to inhale, deeply, through the nose. And then exhale, deeply, through the mouth, until you can hear your heartbeat. I propose that you make every breath last seven seconds. But do what you feel is best for you. Remember to sit comfortably and concentrate. All thoughts should be stopped. Once you reach peace, hear your heartbeat ask yourself inside, "How are you?" Like you are asking another person this question. You will hear your voice in a calm way, and it's the same voice you hear inside yourself when you are reading to yourself. That voice will give you the most honest possible answer, an answer that does not go out of your head. It does, however, come out of your heart. So it is not controlled it is real!

Please, do it. Do this *breathing* exercise. It should last as long as the video you are listening to. And then come back to continue this flight with me.

Now how did you feel after the exercise? If you did it well you should have been in the Alpha state of mind, that complete purifying state that calms down your system. Did you get an answer to your question? Some of us do, and some don't. At least not always the first time around. But please, if you didn't, just keep practicing. It is a matter of practice and how we are connected with ourselves. We are human beings, remember, and not just physical, but also of a spiritual existence. And as the most perfect beings on this world, we must stay aware of this. We are perfection and magnificence but we must know what to do with it! This exercise was not even a deep meditation, however. But it is a very important basic breathing exercise that we must repeat until we get an answer to our question.

In each of us lives a child who we were, and it cries out for our love and attention. When you accept yourself and when you start to love yourself just the way you are, you come to a state of gratitude. From a state of gratitude, you project positive thoughts. Positive thoughts create positive energy. And positive energy attracts positive people, situations and events. And this is the path to happiness. It is that easy and obvious. This is why you have to make this inner connection. You can also ask yourself a different question. The one we've asked here is just the easiest one. But don't give up if you don't get the answer right away. It is because you are not aware of your inner self yet. And it is afraid of scaring you and at the same time it is scared of you. Why? Because for years you didn't recognize it and you didn't pay attention to it. So be calm and persistent and you will see the progress. How is this connected to our goals and happiness? Well, we are going step by step, remember? So everything will become clear. I will give my best to be so, I promise.

But let me explain what occurred during this exercise.

What happens when we breathe so deeply? Oxygen in large quantities enters our body, right? What happens then? Our brain receives a greater amount of oxygen. Our heart receives a larger amount of oxygen, and this leads to oxidation and detoxification of our body. Did you know that in 1926 Otto Heinrich Warburg discovered that cancer cells can only live in the body in which exists a lack of oxygen? In 1931 he won the Nobel Prize for this! So, all we need is more oxygen in our body, right?

So why don't we learn this in school? Well, who will buy industrialized food and water if we knew it isn't good for us? And that it is extremely detrimental to our health and eventually we will need pharmaceutical drugs to survive in our later years if we continue to consume such unhealthy substances. Who would buy pharmaceutical drugs if we were healthy? Right? Google this and find out what is happening out there and how you can get more oxygen in your body. It can be done by natural water, mountain air, deep breathing, and you can also make a "base environment" of your body from utilizing baking soda (sodium hydrogen carbonate: $NaHCo3$). These are just suggestions for you so you can obtain more information to assist in the healthy maintenance of your body.

And what happens with our brain when more oxygen comes? The brain says, "Oh finally, now I can work and do so with more capacity! You finally stopped the negative thoughts that you were poisoning me with. You finally came back to yourself, to your heart and to me. Yes! Now I can be creative and function at full capacity. Now I can give you the clear thinking and incisive ideas that will make your life better."

Your brain is happy now because we just did another very important thing: We gave our body more oxygen and begin to establish a healthier system!

It is this easy. Try it and you will see. Do that exercise every night before you go to sleep, and see what happens. When you learn this, you can go into meditation deeper and deeper each time and the results will be more and more satisfying. You will feel better, you will be focused, you will reduce stress, you will find peace in yourself and that New You will work better, do better and be better. And if you set goals and go in your direction by doing what you love, nothing can stop you. The sky will be the limit! I don't promise this to you. You have to promise this to yourself. Because nothing will happen if you don't do the exercise and use the techniques and formulas that I will show you!

During the exercise, were you able to think about nothing? If yes, you are one of the few. Usually we have so many things on our mind that it is very hard to stop them. Have you heard of the chakras? Those are the energy centers in the body. There are seven of them.

I will not tell you about all of them now because in this moment, connected to this subject, for us the seventh chakra is important, for it is responsible for the mind. It is the point on the top of our head. Put your palm on it, concentrate and feel the pulse. So, if our thoughts fly about uncontrolled, you just think about this chakra and it will stop them. This, too, needs to be practiced. But it is very useful when you need to be calm. If you are in the stressful meeting and you can't get out, or in any situation that you need to be focused, do it just for few minutes. Later on you will need just half of a minute, or a few seconds, and you will benefit from it; a lot, believe me.

So, our mind can be controlled? Well, yes, of course. We are the masters of our mind; it is not vice versa. And those 2% of people who have 90% wealth of the world, mentioned at the beginning here, know this, and also know that 98% of others don't know it. So they use us in the system of achieving their own goals. But now it's time to wake up! All of us 98%. Wake up to find our own way and reorder that percentage of wealth. There is enough for all of us from Mother Nature.

So after this experience, are some people really born under a lucky star, or they know something that others don't? It is obvious that they do. I've studied this since 2008, in the works of many authors, the experience of millions of people around the world and it is my pleasure to share my knowledge with you today, because you gave me your time by reading this book, and your time is the most valuable resource in your life. So, thank you and if you like this stay here, there is so much more.

So, after the exercise, did you feel anything? One side of the brain is responsible for the information and facts, but what about other side of the brain that stores the knowledge of our emotions? Yes, you read this correctly. Knowledge of emotions! Emotions, huh? Perhaps you suspected this already? Well, *we need to know the emotions in us. This is the key*! People often have that superficially look about their emotions. Yet, if they are sad, they cry. If they are scared, they step aside and hide. But in fact emotions are our **greatest power**!

Our emotions are here to stay. So remember this: they indicate whether you are in compliance with yourself. Are you at peace? If not, then ask yourself why not and what can you do to change this? For our emotions are here for us. One reason so that we can recognize our responsibility for the situation which we are in, and to act in order to change that situation if it's not good for us. Sadness is not there to be mourned, grieved and spent in depression. Sadness is there for us to grow through a particular situation and to continue to become stronger. How? Each person that appears in our life appears in order to teach us a lesson. Our experience is the best teacher.

People learn the best from their own experiences. What I am attempting here is to show you that you can feel why you are not okay, but that you have to act in order to change it. And this can be done also by learning from other people's experiences. But do not waste your time over trying to find something that has already been found. Ask the one who knows, and then find something greater, and become extraordinary! Even negative things in life bring lessons and important changes. And without change there is no progress! Very often when we look back, we are most grateful to those difficult situations because they showed us what is beautiful in life.

Emotions give you a sign asking: are you going in the right direction! If you feel happy and excited, that's good path, stay on it. If you're feeling anxiety, discomfort, sadness, depression, frustration, then it's time to say STOP and dedicate yourself to five minutes of reflection or meditation so you can find out what is going on. Then the process can begin, and you can start THE CHANGE.

If you are not feeling good, you can't be better in what you do. If you are not okay then you can't help anyone else, and you can't progress.

The Dalai Lama said, *"Everyone wants a happy life without difficulties or suffering. We create many of the problems we face. No one intentionally creates problems, but we tend to be slaves to powerful emotions like anger, hatred and attachment that are based on misconceived projections about people and things. We need to find ways of reducing these emotions by eliminating the ignorance that underlies them and applying opposite forces. "*

And what is the opposite force? Yes, you are right, those are positive emotions that create positive energy and attract positive life events, people, and situations in our life, as I already mentioned.

One good technique to get to the positive state of mind is the technique that Brian Tracy explained, and it is called **"The magic wand."** Imagine that you hold a magic wand that will turn your situation into the perfect one. Wave it and it is perfect. And you stop to see how everything looks. Wave it again and now imagine what it would look like if the situation is perfect. Visualize it with as much details as you can. Immediately alter the state. That's it.

And what happens when you get to the inner You, when

you identify emotions and make contact with yourself? Then you ask yourself the **key question *"What is my goal?"*** The answer is inside you. The same voice that gave you the answer to "How are you?" will give you answer to the most important question of all! And then action steps onto the stage! You will read more about this in Happiness formula latter on.

So, how we can achieve all this?

Rhonda Byrne, author of the international bestseller The Secret, and her book The Power, as well as a movie production of The Secret (which has changed the lives of millions of people around the world) said: *"Anything that anyone desires is because they think their desire will make them happy. But remember that happiness is a state inside of us, and something on the outside can only bring fleeting happiness. Permanent happiness comes from you choosing to be permanently happy. When you choose happiness, then you attract all the happy things as well. The happy things are the icing on the cake, but the cake is happiness..."*

This lady changed my life! So I am very grateful to her. I would like to meet her and hug her and say, "Thank you very, very, very much!" But now I am going to tell you my story, and from my heart. In 2008 my body was operating on a minimum energy capacity. My immunity was low. My heart was weak. The nerve endings in my feet were weakened and I was no longer me. I didn't have the strength to walk. I was attacked by the Coxsackie virus and it demolished my body because doctors found it too late. At this time, one doctor sad to me, "Your condition is very bad. You have to come to a hospital and we will examine you, but according to this results, you have a year or maybe a year and a half left to live." What? Live but a year and a half longer--tops? Me!? No way!

You can't tell me this! I refused to accept it. But then my mom got sick and I had to also fight for her as well as for myself. After all this occurred, I started going online and researching everything I could about viruses on the Internet. I often felt tired and just wanted to sleep forever. But then, there it was. On my computer, the movie The Secret. I actually had bought it two years earlier but never watched it. I know now I should have watched it when I first got it. For when I finally did watch it, what the movie contained totally revived me. So perhaps I would never have been sick if I had watched it two years earlier!

Remember this: Nothing comes to us by accident! There is always a reason. Please start to pay attention to that. Every detail is important. Follow the details, be curious, and you will win! You will be excellent! You will be the change and the miracle of your life!

Back to my story: Doctors had forbidden me physical activity, but I went with friends to the fitness center and did my exercises, although very slowly. I then changed my eating habits and visited Monastery Ostrog in Montenegro for few days, to find peace. I saw myself as a happy and healthy person again in my mind. I became thankful for my life, for my husband, for everything that is good on Earth. I was even thankful for the virus because it showed me the best way to look at life, how to believe in myself and how to be stronger. I then would ask every night for the virus to release my body, like I was talking to another person. I was praying every day, at my home and the monks at the monastery prayed for me. I was doing interesting and pleasant things: watching comedies, singing, painting, writing poems, etc. Then my recovery came. And the doctors couldn't believe it! All the new results showed that I was just fine! And here I am in front of you now, today, eight years after my ordeal. And I am doing what I love the most, telling you the story that has changed my life. Telling it in order to give you ideas how you can change your own, and telling it in order to help you and give you the best of me. I have never been healthier! And I know very well now what I want out of life. But I experienced something that "hit me in the head" and woke me up.

So do not wait until something hits you! Wake up now!

I am not telling you not to use your medicament. I used mine. Or not to go to a doctor. I went to mine. I am just telling you to get to know the law of attraction. It will help you to see how the system works and then to use it in the best way.

The **Law of Attraction** works no matter if you believe it or not. I believe, because I am alive, thanks to it!

Are you ready for the most important decision in your life?

Decide to be happy!

Happiness is a state of mind. Have you seen a child who is depressed? Of course you haven't.

How it is possible? Train your happiness. Yes, you read that right. You can learn and train for happiness as well as everything else in life.

1. Laugh every day for five minutes, without any reason, then repeat it for 21 days straight and it will become your habit to do.

2. Listen, or even better play the music you love.

3. *Think of someone you love.*

4. *Think of your pet if you have it; pets are a source of positive energy.*

5. The biggest sources of positive energy are ***babies.*** Think of the baby you love. You know how kids feel when someone is positive and just wants to be with them? That's how it feels if our soul is awakened.

6. ***Be thankful*** to the people who inspire you. In this book you will read who are those people to me I should be thankful for. Even I don't know some of them. Yet their word, work and energy came to me, to teach me, to show me, to open a new door for me, as I am doing with all my heart for you right now. Even if there is only one person who reads this, I am so happy to do this, and thankful, too, that I might positively touch and make but a few positive changes in her/his life, this change that will bring happiness. That is the only reason I am writing this book. I wish you will be thankful to yourself because you read this book. Not to me, but to yourself. Please, because I am thankful to you for giving me your time now.

Are you ready to make the decision? Are you ready to wake up? Great! Then take action! Remember the frog? Don't hold on decision.

Play the same video I gave you for breathing exercise. But now only watch it, feel it and live it.

And now the crucial:

When you establish emotional balance you need to establish a balance between your heart and mind. What do I want/wish? How can I achieve it? The first is an emotional job, the second is mental. And then you can use all those techniques about management, problem solving, prioritization, etc.

This is why my point of view is different!

Other schools teach you mental or emotional techniques. I would like to show you that we have to use emotional techniques first and then implement all mental techniques we know, then the system will be healthy. Otherwise it would be like you want to plant a tree in toxic ground. Even if it grows it will be sickly. And also, these two parts of our growth can't be separated, otherwise you will be happy or successful, but not happy and successful.

Do you agree with me? If you do, then it is time to change your perspective.

Find out what you feel and do whatever you have to do to feel good. This is the only way. When you feel good, you are the healthy ground and everything positive that you plant in your mind or your soul will grow healthy and you will be successful and satisfied and happy.

Is it clear now? I hope it is. If you use all your skills and techniques to achieve the goals of others you're just build their dream. But you need to build yours! So start now!

Live your own dream!

And what is the conclusion at the end of this chapter? How can we be successful and happy at the same time? We can if we make *balance*.

Now, I present you the ***LHM SUCCESS FORMULA!***

S – "Set your own goals."

U – "U are the only one who knows what is best for yourself. Find it IN you."

C – "Create your own peace and find out what are your desires."

C – "Create an action plan, set time limit and do it! Reach it! Live it!"

E – "Excellence exists in you. Be the excellence."

S – "Sense your feelings and listen to them. Do whatever it takes to feel good."

S – "Stick to it. Act. Do it! If you fail, do it again and again. Try and try and try. No one has succeeded something big in the first attempt."

There has never been a better chance for us than right now to become a creative power in this world, with the most success, the highest income and a happy life. Let's make this world a better place together!

Now, I have a special gift for you: ***THE LHM BALANCE ALGORITHM!***

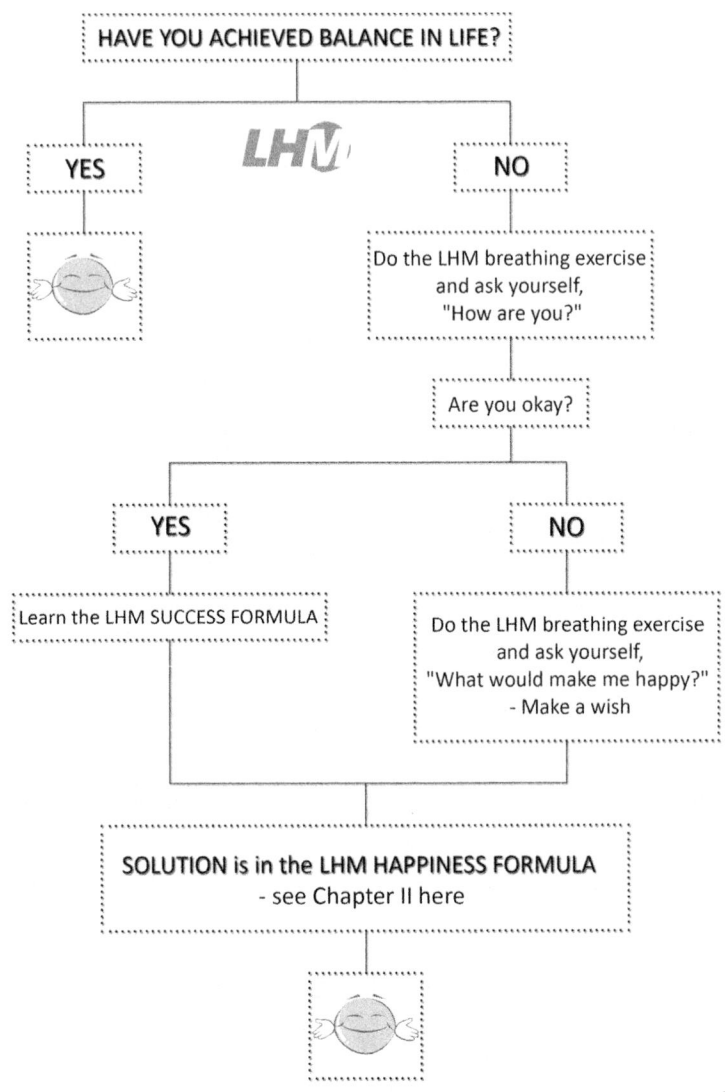

Exercise: For the meaning of every letter of **SUCCESS**, make your own association drawings. This way you will better remember the meanings, you will remember them longer than you even expected, and you will know how to use this formula with no special effort. But have fun! For life is fun!

S ....

U ....

C ....

C ....

E ....

S ....

S ....

Exercise: Make your own association drawings for the
LHM BALANCE ALGORITHM

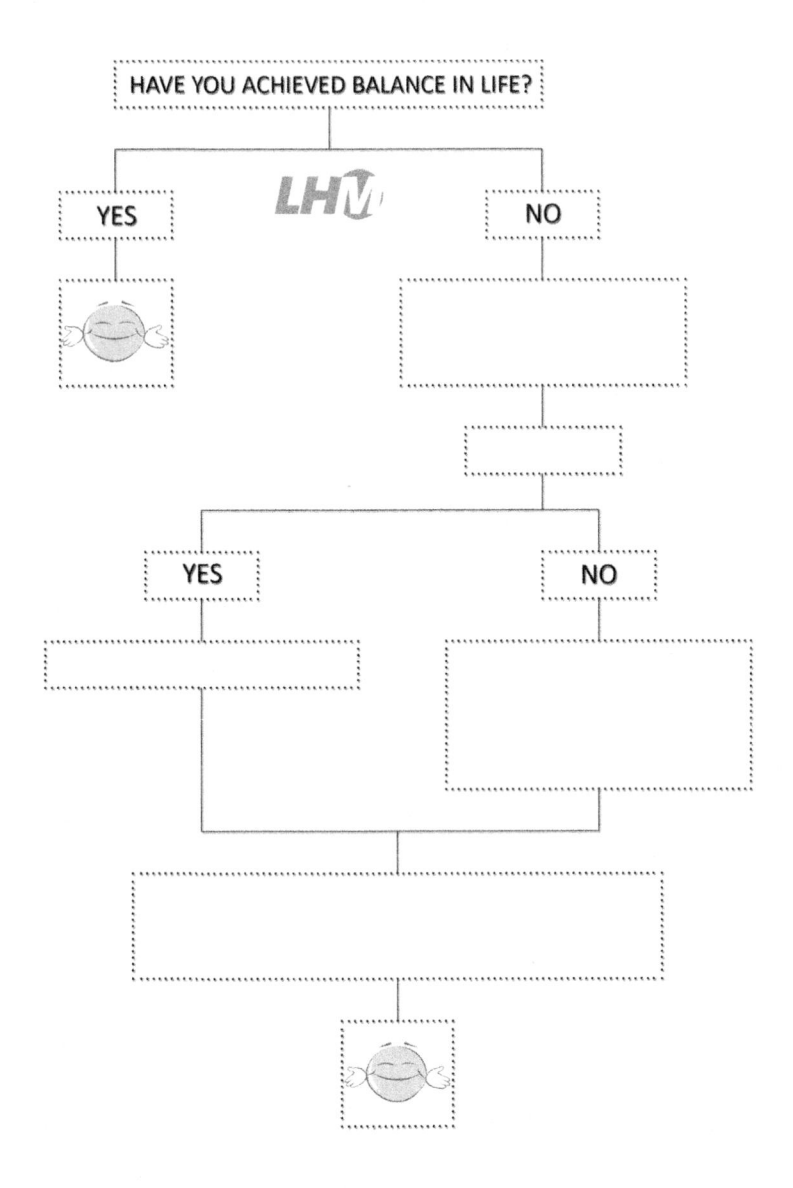

HAVE YOU ACHIEVED BALANCE IN LIFE?

YES / NO

YES / NO

1. LHM IQ Training Question: What is common to a snowflake, cow and forefinger?

. . . .

CHAPTER 2

HAPPINESS

"Happiness depends upon ourselves."

~ Aristotle

What really is happiness? Is it just a feeling or a state of mind? We have decided to be happy. So, it is a state of mind. Happiness is the happiest state of mind! And we will act that way in order to achieve satisfaction and success.

Some people believe in a bright future. They think positively and life leads to Love. They are smiling and cheerful. It seems that they have everything they want.

Are their desires small or they are "Gods of reachable small things," satisfied and grateful for what they have?

Some people perceive the worst possible outcome, so if it does happen, it happened, and they "knew" that it would. Most likely, they will say, "See, I've told you so." Apparently they are proud and egocentric, but they are really unhappy, sad, lonely and without love.

Are their desires too big or they are "Gods of unreachable big things," unsatisfied and ungrateful with what they have?

Which side is better?

I believe we should be grateful for what we have at this moment. Start with a small goal, reach it and become a "God of small things." Be grateful. Than push up your goal, reach it and become a "God of bigger things." Then make it small for you again. But be grateful. Then reach the next goal and your way will become limitless.

But if you start with a big goal and you don't succeed several times in a row, how will you feel? Maybe some of us get more strength from that and do it until we succeed. But most of us just quit, right?

The suggestion is to start with a small goal and rise from it. Even the longest road begins with the first step. And though you are not a bird to glide, at least you will not overfly the road. You only have to go one step after another.

Many things, in our lives make us happy. For some of us, happiness is being in love, for others it is in family, or in abundance, or in success, or in whatever brings a smile upon our faces and peace in our hearts and minds.

Every man is the magnificence at his own shape, perfection one of a kind. You are perfection. He, she is perfection. I am perfection.

Maybe you wonder: How can it be if we are so different? It can because perfection doesn't exist. It is not real. We are the best versions of ourselves. That is perfect enough.

All of us individually, different things, situations, events and actions make happy. Wouldn't it be great if there existed a Special Power which would connect people by those things that make them happy? Then we would easily find someone who suits us, the one who has the same desires, the same goals the same opinions, and we will merge our lives into one successful, happy life. It would be perfect! Everyone would be happy in love and in life.

But life doesn't work that way.

Life can be an unexpected set of events, and it demands tolerance and a lot of friendship and love from us. Otherwise, where would be the excitement of life if we all know our way from birth to the end? How would we grow and what would we learn if we were the same or if we spend the most time with people that are just like us? Would we really be happy? Or just our ego would be happy because it is self-satisfied?

This is very important: make a difference between your *soul-self* and your *ego-self*. Love is pure and unconditional.

Love is a state of your soul-self. But if expectations exist in relationships, then this is not love. It is ego-self who wants to be satisfied.

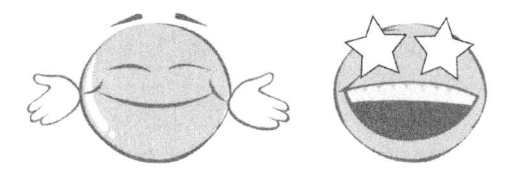

If you want to be happy, your job is to live from your soul-self, to love unconditionally and don't expect anything.

Yes, of course, it is hard, but it can be learned and it is a road to soul freedom!

Imagine two persons who really ***love each other unconditionally***. They believe in each other without suspicion and without jealousy. They live life with each other, but in their own uniqueness. Isn't that great? You may be thinking that is just imagination. But no! That is how love should be! Love from soul-self. Every other kind of love comes from ego-self and you have to overcome it!

I tell you unconditional love exists! I live that love with my husband. He is always here for me. Remember when I was sick? We lived in a building with no elevator, so he carried me to and from the second floor in his arms. He was home while I was at seminars and conferences and never once complained and never showed jealousy. And I am always here for him.

I helped him while he was studying for college. I didn't go to parties. I stayed home with him and wrote this book. I was helping him myself to finish college and to find a job. I was home taking care of everything while he was on business trips. We never looked at each other's mobile phones or social network accounts or email. We just believe each other and have absolute trust. He has authorization to my bank account as I have to his. We have this kind of connection even after 12 years of life together. And I smile every time I see him, and it is vice versa. But I had a near-death experience, remember? I wasn't this kind of understanding and loving person before.

A great power from unfortunate circumstances can make a stronger connection between people and keep our hearts pure and loyal.

Don't wait for something bad to happen or to lose someone to see what you had! Live this moment in the present as it is! Don't go to the past or too far into the future. Be just here and live just this. The present is only thing that we have. For the past is gone and the future does not yet exist.

People who really love someone don't try to change that person. They love that person just as he/she is. We must understand that we can't change somebody and we don't even have right to do so.

The only one who can be changed by me is me. I have a power to change myself. To choose which way to go. To choose people in my life, except family of course. And most important: To choose my reactions to those people. But I can't change someone else. It is a waste of time.

Love is an unconditional state with no expectations. Though being in love is something completely different.

Like Osho said: *"If you love a flower, don't pick it up, because if you pick it up, it dies. And it ceases to be what you love. So, if you love a flower, let it be. Love is not about the possession. Love is about appreciation."*

Well, we are again on the same point: appreciation! Appreciate what you have and be grateful for it!

Here is a little exercise for you that will change your life!

Take a notebook.

1. On the left side write your wishes, but in a form of goals.

A well-written goal has to pass the SMART mechanism:

> **S**pecific
>
> **M**easurable
>
> **A**chievable
>
> **R**ealistic
>
> **T**imely

For example, if today is 01-01-2017 and you weigh 75 kg, the goal can be:

Goal: On 05-05-2017 I weigh 65 kg.

Specific means that you wrote exactly what you will achieve. But what is very important: you wrote it in PRESENT tense, like you already have the result.

Measurable means that you can measure your weight and see if you have done it.

Achievable means that you are going to lose 10 kg in four months and that it is possible.

Realistic means that it is real. It is possible.

Timely means that you have set an exact deadline.

SMART

After setting the goal, write your plan. How are you going to achieve it? What are the actions required? Every action is a new goal. Make prioritization of actions and do it!

What I would like to add to the SMART technique is that you have to feel that you already achieved it. Close your eyes and visualize, for example, how you look like with 65 kg. And try to imagine situations when people come to you and say to you how you look nice, how you are attractive. Feel that thought. Live it! And you will have it!

> **F**eel that visualization!
>
> **L**ive that feeling!
>
> **Y**ou will do it!

You can remember this by association:

FLY SMART = Imagine that you are a pilot on a plane. And even if you are smart, if you don't fly smart you are going to hit the ground.

This is a place where mind takes over from heart. Associations are the best technique for remembering. Not repetition, associations. When you represent to yourself some definition or whatever you have to remember with association pictures, you will remember it easier and you will use it with no effort. So, you may remember plane and phone, then you will immediately know that is FLY SMART.

2. On the right side of the notebook write "gratitude" sentences like you already have what you wish for and you are grateful for having it.

For example:

I am very grateful and satisfied now, when I weigh 65 kg.

As the time passes, and if you act by your action plan, you will see how goals become reality and disappear from the left side and go to the right side, where you are really grateful for what you have. It is fantastic feeling when you see that. You will feel great! Then set new goals and reach them too!

Every night before you go to bed say, "Thank you" for everything in your life, even if it is just having eyes to see.

From this state of gratitude you will come to the state of having, because you will attract more and more better things. The message that you send the Universe is that you are satisfied, and the Universe will respond with more things to be grateful and satisfied for. If you are not grateful, if you are just complaining, the Universe won't understand. It will just give you more and more things that you have been thinking about. So, if you are complaining about bills, the Universe gives you more bills, because it doesn't make a difference in the content and intent of your thoughts. But if you talk how you always find a parking place, then you will always find a parking space. Because Universe hears this and gives it to you.

For example (I tested this in my everyday situations), I say to myself, "Every time I take the bus the closest seated person there get ups and gives me his seat." And he does. It is joke among my friends now. Pay attention on your sentence construction, however. Use "every time" and present tense. No future tense, because if I say "will," it is future tense. And I will never reach it. For this is about "what" is to happen. Not when. For the future is always off in the distance!

So the grasp the power is in our thoughts. But not every thought. Just those which make us feel something good or something positive or something productive.

Now can you see the connection between thoughts, feelings and what is happening to you?

You produce thoughts. Important thoughts produce feelings. Feelings create emotions. Emotions indicate to us are we on the right track. And that is why we went to the Alpha state of mind with--very important—the breathing exercise, remember? When you feel, you must act in order to make that feeling good or even better or extraordinary, depending on what you felt.

Thought --- Feeling --- Emotion --- Act

T.*F*.E.A *(F in a cup of TEA)*

It is all connected.

The solution is to pay attention on what we think about.

If you think positively, proceed; if you think negatively stop that thought.

The new age philosophy is that we can direct our mind in the new, positive direction.

We must see happiness as a precondition for a nice, rich and successful life. And not a nice, rich and successful life as a precondition for happiness!

If we do what we love, we will do it the best we can. We will give our energy to it and we will become the best. And we will become the necessary experts, and wealth and money will follow our development.

So, happiness depends on what?

As we saw, the key to this whole riddle is to *Feel our Thoughts - F.O.T* (FOoT without the big O).

Listen to a child in your heart. Discover your desires and follow them. Wishes can be small or they can be huge. The most beautiful is to start with small wishes, define them, set goals and find ways to implement these goals. And call forth good thoughts, feelings, and most gentle spice: the Law of Attraction in order to achieve them. The most powerful way to start is with a small goal, and when you reach it you will feel better! Then achieve a larger goal and you will feel much better! Then achieve your dream and you will feel spectacular! This is where happiness lives. And this is where we all should be!

The Law of Attraction is what some people call The Secret. But the secret is in its own simplicity: To want something, then visualize it as if we already have it, then feel it--deeply feel it—and feel the happiness. Then work toward achieving it! Our job is to pick from a catalog of desire, and get it!

Just remember this. For this is very important and something that The Secret doesn't give attention to. But Live from Your Heart and Mind is setting it as crucial!

When you pick a wish, that wish must become a goal! That means that it should be FLY SMART, felt as F.O.T and recognized as the set of activities that you must do. T.F.E.A! Nothing comes without effort. We all are doing things toward reaching and achieving goals.

The only difference between successful and happy people and the others is in fact in answer to this question: Whose goals are you accomplishing? Yours or…? Set your goals, make a plan, set actions and then do it for you. Or someone else will hire you to do it for them!

It's that simple. And happiness will come! Believe me it will! It is already here. Waiting for you to just change your point of view and look inside, not outside. As Aristotle said: *"Happiness depends upon ourselves."* These are the smartest words I have ever heard.

You may see the need for a little self-discipline here. Well, yes. It is all in habits. When these new habits become your lifestyle you will not have to be so self-disciplined, and you will enjoy more. But until then, if you want to reach happiness, you have to be self-disciplined, at least just a little bit.

The main difference between successful people and the other ones is in fact that successful people are focused and they act, they are self-disciplined and work in order to gain the result.

Be successful and when you get it, you can let it. Let the happiness be your lifestyle.

Now, I present you the *LHM HAPPINESS FORMULA*:

1. Take a few minutes for yourself.

2. Find peace inside you and feel your breathing and heartbeat.

3. Ask yourself this simple question "How are you?"

4. Answer from your heart.

5. If the answer is "Great," "Happy," "Satisfied," then you are on the right path. But if the answer is "Unhappy," "Sad," "Lonely" or it is just silence, then you have to ask yourself another question: "What would make you happy?" The answer is your wish.

6. Make a FLY SMART goal from your wish.

7. Feel it as F.O.T

8. Do it as T.F.E.A! Make an action plan and do one by one an action by action. You will reach it! And when you accomplish it, you will feel satisfaction, and satisfaction leads to happiness.

9. Do not stop! Take responsibility of your life and create your happiness.

Now, I have a special gift for you: ***THE LHM HAPPINESS ALGORITHM***!

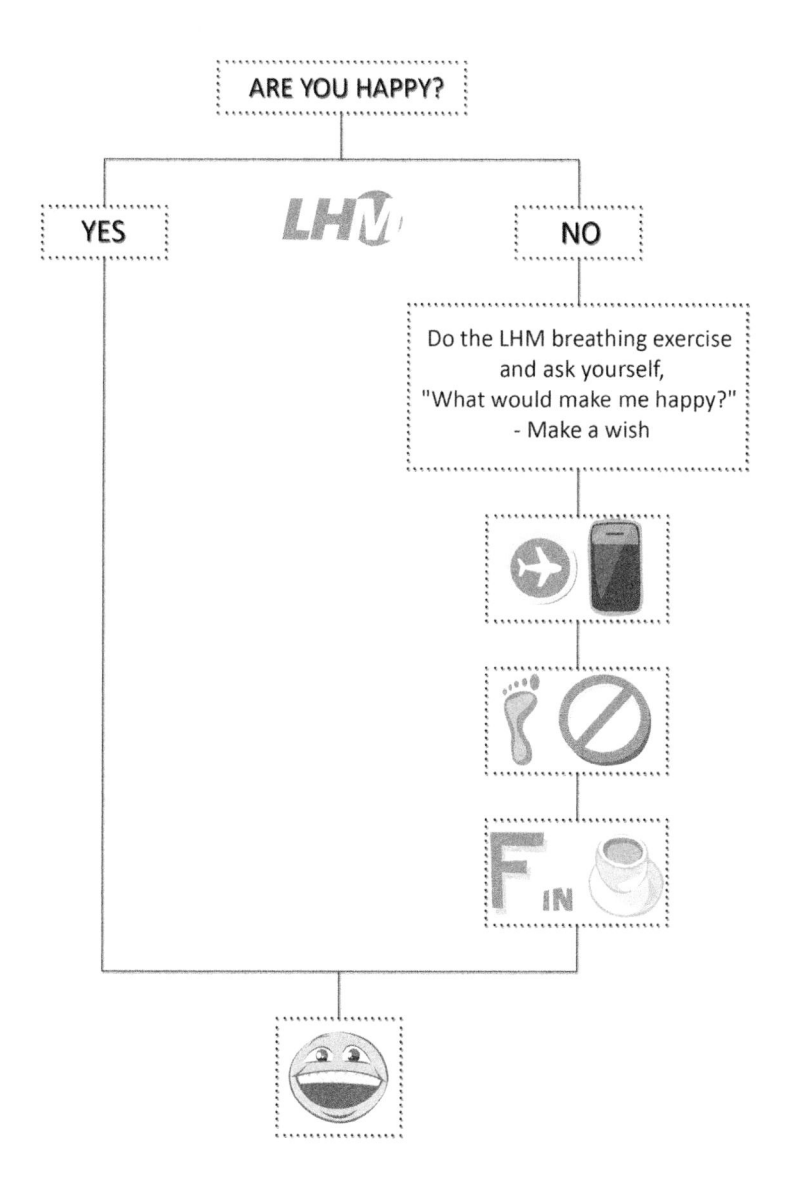

```
                    ARE YOU HAPPY?
                    ┌──────┴──────┐
                  YES             NO
                                   │
                        Do the LHM breathing exercise
                              and ask yourself,
                        "What would make me happy?"
                               - Make a wish
                                   │
                              [✈️  📱]
                                   │
                              [👣  🚫]
                                   │
                              [F_IN  ☕]
                                   │
                    ┌──────────────┘
                    │
                  [😀]
```

Exercise: For meaning of the LHM FLY SMART technique, make your own association drawings.

LHM FLY SMART

. . . .

Exercise: For meaning of the formula Thought --- Feeling --- Emotion --- Act (T.F.E.A), make your own association drawings.

LHM T.F.E.A

. . . .

Exercise: For meaning of the formula Feel Our Thoughts (F.O.T), make your own association drawings.

LHM F.O.T

. . . .

Exercise: For every step of the *LHM HAPPINESS FORMULA*, make your own association drawings.

1. ....

2. ....

3. ....

4. ....

5. ....

6. ....

7. ....

8. ....

9. ....

Exercise: This will become the most valuable paper in your life. Write your 10 SMART Goals.

1. ....

2. ....

3. ....

4. ....

5. ....

6. ....

7. ....

8. ....

9. ....

10. ....

Write 10 gratitude sentences for those 10 SMART Goals.

1. ....

2. ....

3. ....

4. ....

5. ....

6. ....

7. ....

8. ....

9. ....

10. ....

Exercise: Make your own association drawings for the ***LHM HAPPINESS ALGORITHM***.

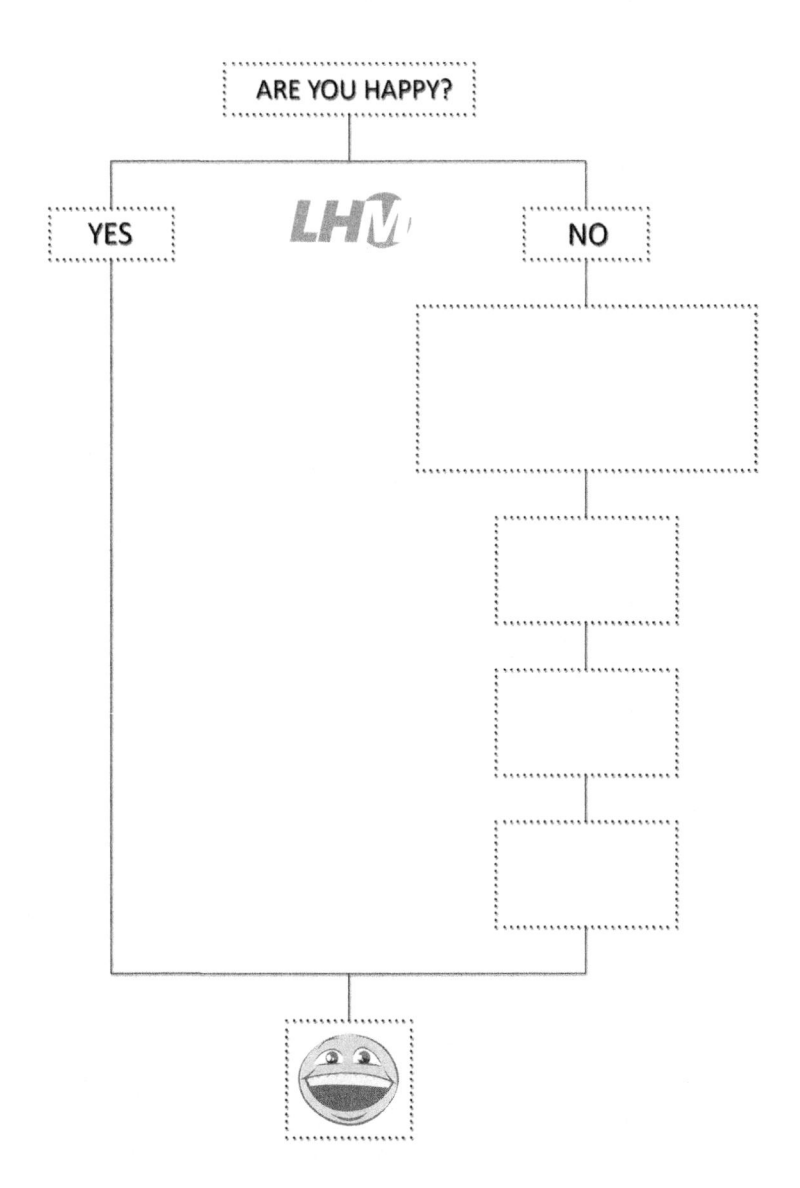

Use F.O.T and T.F.E.A. on every goal. Really feel every thought. If you feel well about a goal, then that is it! Make an action plan for it and do it! Feel satisfaction as you are doing it, it will lead you to happiness! If you don't feel well, then change a goal which is not good for you.

2. LHM IQ Training Question: What is common to the water in Australia and the planet Venus?

....

CHAPTER 3

BELIEF

"Believe you can and you're halfway there."

~ Theodore Roosevelt

Let's make a brief but little detour from previous subjects, and ask ourselves this question: What do we really know about anything?

Everything that is proven, even scientifically, is proven based on previous evidences, or maybe somebody's previous knowledge. And, hypothetically, if we track it back, step by step, through history, wouldn't we end up to the first fact that was a base for the first research? So let me ask you a question: Who set that fact? Humans did. So, is it possible that the fact is actually just another hypothesis and that Socratic paradox: *"I know that I know nothing"* is actually the most valuable fact?

I am not trying to make proven things unproven. I am just trying to show that there is a lot in this world that we don't know. And the only, I would say, smart thing, that we can do, is to use what we know in order to make this life easier, happier and more beautiful for us. The system of life that exists today is created by us. By that I mean that humans created buildings, cars, computers, industry, law, money etc. People have made this kind of life and learn how to live in it. But, really, the most important question is unsolved: What happens when we die?

The point is: ***The secret*** is all that was. The secret is all there is. The secret is all that will ever be. No matter how hard we try to understand how things work and why they occur, we will understand it only within the limits of our own minds. To understand more, we have to expand our minds. And, we will do that with our LHM IQ training questions at the end of every chapter.

Until that expanding happens, we just need to use the best that there is. Use your time for yourself, make your life beautiful and make order in your home first. How can you fix your life if your locker is a mess?

Now, maybe you wonder: What does this have to do with happiness or success?

This is one of the main points: Nothing happen without a reason. Everything is relative and there is always a way!

Sometimes when something unexpected happens, people say: "Who knows why this is good." But it seems to me that this sentence is unfounded. I believe that we manage ourselves, our lives, our happiness. *We write the novel of our lives,* and not vice versa.

When I say "belief" or "faith," it doesn't mean an explicit definition of religious faith. I think the faith in yourself, as a deep respect for your own personality.

I am the only one who is responsible for whatever is happening to me.

I know this is a hard thing to accept. People usually blame other people or "inexplicable forces" for what happened in their lives. But if we just stop for a moment and admit that in every situation is at least a little bit our own responsibility, and just fix it, wouldn't this be a better world to live in?

I apologize to those who have been in situation that is out of their hands. I was too, and I understand.

You know, I survived the bombing of my country, so I know how it feels to be powerless. I am from a country in Europe that not so long ago suffered a great war. But I will not talk about war. I will just ask you to imagine this: Kids go to school. And in school their teachers say that they must go back home because the air force bombing of our country is going to start that day. But we were kids, we didn't understand how serious it was. We were even happy at first because we got to go home early. But when it started, it was hard just to bear the sound of it and cope with the fear and horror of it. Can you imagine how it felt to huddle in a cold, dark basement all day long? We didn't know if we were going to survive that day. I was just a kid back in 1999, but I felt like a target.

My family, friends and I huddled in fear. And I would shiver every time I heard a plane fly over, or when the siren began to sound, warning us of the approaching danger. I didn't do anything wrong. My family and friends didn't do anything wrong. Yet we were all in the same predicament and dealing with the same persistent problem: How to survive!? It is impossible to make choices and write a novel about your life in such moments and during such a time. You don't have the choice! But you must be strong and positive and pray for your life every single day. For the only thing you have is your mind, and hope.

However, you can do extraordinary things with your mind, even in moments such as these. I would see myself happy again in my mind. And picture myself running in the woods for pleasure, swimming in a beautiful blue sea or singing and dancing at concerts. Even in that cold, dark basement we would play with shadows from the candles, and we would sing and dance. Sometimes we pretended we were eating cookies, even when it was just a slice of old, musty bread with a little bit of salt. I remember now that my grandfather had planted potatoes, beans and onions in our garden instead of flowers, and how happy we were to have something fresh to eat and which was not humanitarian aid.

You have probably heard of Novak Djokovic, the world's number one tennis player on the ATP list, or of Ana Ivanovic who was number one on the WTA list and also one of the most beautiful women on the World. They are both from my country. Well, Novak was also a child during the war and spent considerable time with friends and family huddled in a cold, dark basement. Meanwhile, Ana practiced tennis in an empty swimming pool during those days. But look at them now! So, successful world athletes! For all of us during this horrendous period in our country's history believed and knew that the war had to pass one day. And it did, it passed.

Unfortunately, a lot of innocent people didn't survive the war, and I pray God is with their souls. No one has the right to take lives, especially not innocent lives, and especially not children's lives! We are born here on planet Earth to live in peace and love. And we have to share Love. The more love we share, the more love our lives will know. And the less there will be of war and all that's wrong with the world it brings. As it is, every war for a smart and loving people is one that is lost, even before it started. I survived the war in my country, but with a huge scar on my heart. Yet from all the horror and fear I experienced I gained strength and self-confidence and also learned one of life's most important lessons:

Everything is temporarily. Everything is relative. Don't make the mistake of thinking that you have unlimited time. Be aware that you don't know when the end of your life will come. And thus live your life like every day is your last. Use and give from each day to the most important people in your life and for the most important things. Let these be things that you love. And help others. Be generous. Be kind. Be grateful for what you have. And share love and happiness. Therefore, let us stop all negativity and invite only positivity into our lives. Don't be afraid to share love and don't be afraid to receive it. Love will not hurt when it is from our hearts and souls!

"There can be miracles when you believe."

You have to believe in your bright future. No matter what. For then your future will be bright! Look at me. As you can see, war and poverty and illness are defeated by the power of positive thoughts. And by the faith and light direction we manifest in our minds. Just look at Novak and Ana!

If we can, you can!

Here is a quick exercise for you if you find yourself in hard times and think you have a problem of monumental importance. Just stand in front of a mirror, look yourself in the face and ask this question: "What would this problem and my life mean to people two hundred years from now?" Then smile, because you will quickly realize that the answer is "nothing." You will feel a great weight taken off your shoulders when you realize that there is no problem so great and no need to stress. For there is nothing that is as important as you are to yourself.

If you feel you have a serious problem, then ask yourself if there is anything you can do to solve it? If you can't solve it presently why should you stress over it? It is better for you to do something that will make you feel better. If you can solve your problem, then find out what you can do. Then, as we explained, make this a goal to do. Then do it. Solve it, and it will go away. Just have faith and believe in yourself.

The law of attraction is not so secret. Its simple secret lies in the belief that something is achievable and that it will become reality. If we want something, we have to set it as a FLY SMART goal, feel it as F.O.T., analyze possible ways of achieving that goal, define an action plan, do it as T.F.E.A and simply believe in it. It becomes inevitable realization when we do it this way. But also it is important that the goal is not Machiavellian crowned (hidden in some negative motive), that it is positive and that we truly believe that we can make it happen.

As you can see, such belief is another secret ingredient of success and happiness.

But there are things that we often forget. We forget to see what we have and to say "Thank you!" for what we have. We forget to strive for bigger and more beautiful things, and that those things will follow us and will come to us. Usually when this happens, we then start to believe in miracles. But this is not such a miracle. It is simply the next logical step created as a result of our thoughts, feelings, beliefs and actions.

The only miracle in this world is life! You have only one life. So make it a memorable one!

Only we, who know exactly what we want out of life, believe that we can do it. Thus working in this direction can reach pure success and happiness. For we love the world around us and the world loves us. So be one of us—a person successful and happy in the same time!

No matter how, no matter why, it is important that we know want we want, to feel like we already have it and to love and believe in ourselves above all else. Then the path will lead us to find exactly what we are looking for. Life is here for us to enjoy and succeed at, and to be happy and satisfied. Therefore, have faith in it.

I believe, therefore I am.

Now, I present you the ***LHM STRENGTH FORMULA***:

1. Believe in yourself, there is nothing that you can't do.

2. Have faith in life, nothing is happening without a reason.

3. If you are in hard times, ask yourself: "What would this problem and my life mean to people two hundred years from now?"

4. From every difficult situation you will learn and grow, and you must keep this in your mind. The most difficult lessons are for the best. Be the best! Don't be afraid and you will win!

5. "You are your own limit." The Universe is in your mind. Expand your mind with your soul, and the whole Universe will expand for you.

6. If you want something, set it as a goal; analyze possible ways of achieving that goal, and believe in all the activities carried out to achieve that goal; for it is an inevitable realization when you make the action!

7. Get strength from every lost.

8. Grow with life.

LIVE FROM YOUR HEART AND MIND 75

Now, I have a special gift for you: *THE LHM NO PROBLEM ALGORITHM!*

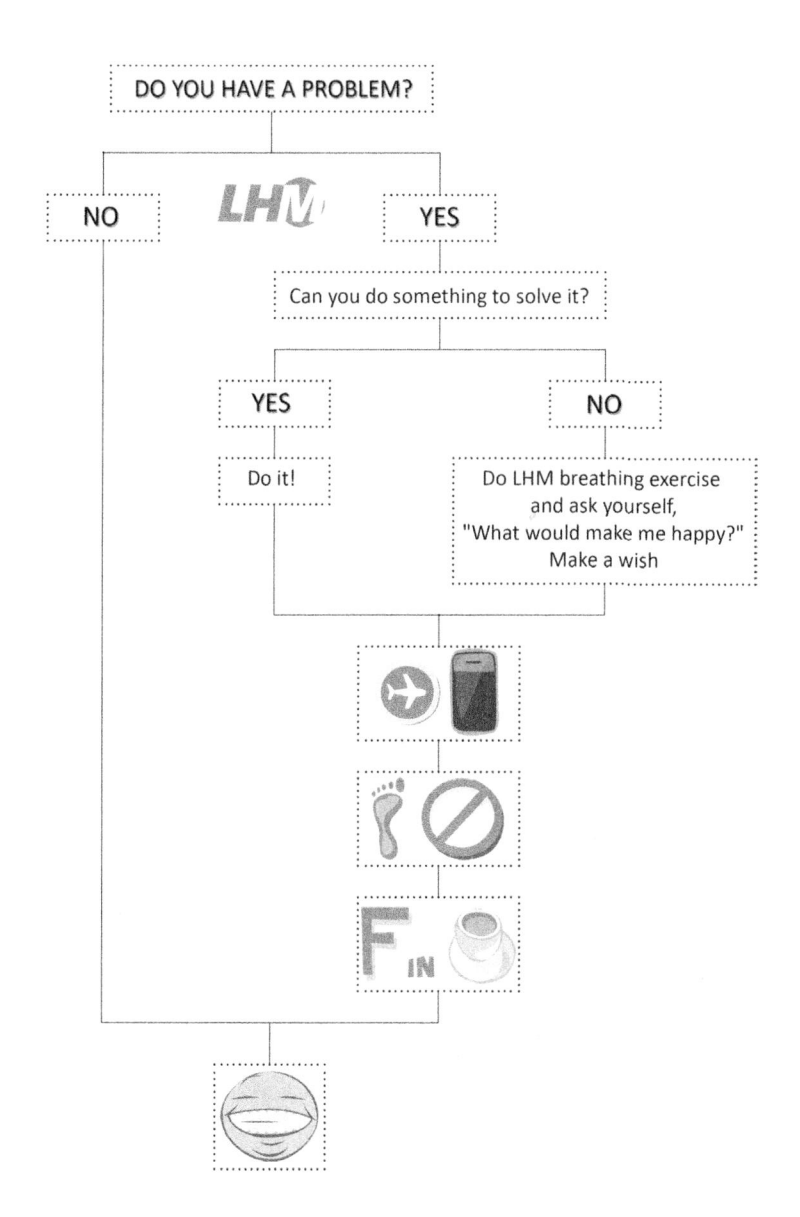

```
                    DO YOU HAVE A PROBLEM?
                    ┌──────────┴──────────┐
                   NO                    YES
                                          │
                            Can you do something to solve it?
                            ┌──────────────┴──────────────┐
                           YES                            NO
                            │                              │
                          Do it!              Do LHM breathing exercise
                                              and ask yourself,
                                              "What would make me happy?"
                                              Make a wish
```

Exercise: For every step of the *LHM STRENGTH FORMULA* make your own association drawings.

1. ....

2. ....

3. ....

4. ....

5. ....

6. ....

7. ....

8. ....

Exercise: Make your own association drawings for the ***LHM NO PROBLEM ALGORITHM***.

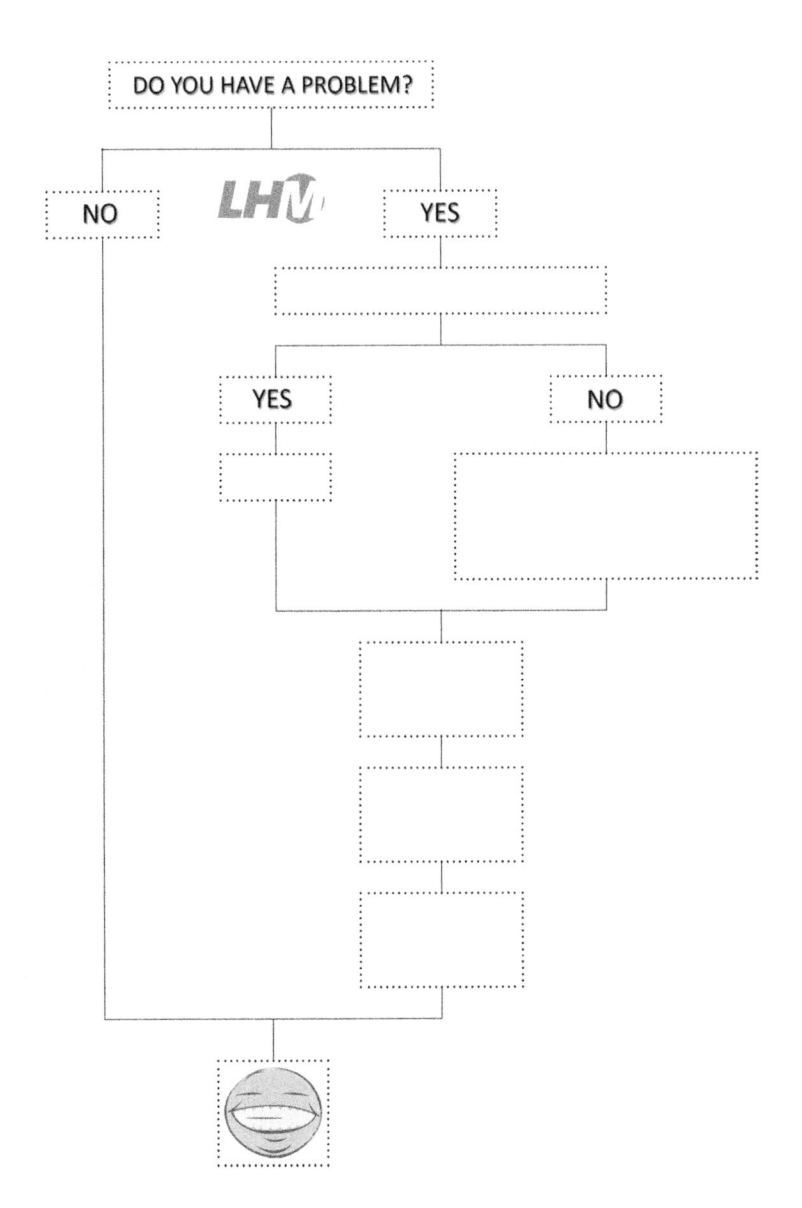

3. LHM IQ Training Question: If we suppose that all creatures on Earth can think and make decisions, what creature thinks from its head, even when it makes decisions from the heart?

• •

CHAPTER 4

OBSTACLES

"Obstacles don't have to stop you. If you run into a wall, don't turn around and give up. Figure out how to climb it, go through it, or work around it."

~ Michael Jordan

A few days after I wrote Chapter 3, something unbelievable happened in my life, and I needed to stop writing and manage several very big, unexpected, life problems. And after a while, come back to "pen and paper," in order to share my experience with you. It was like The Life, as a great teacher, said to me: "Okay now, smart one, here are real problems. Solve them! Use now what you have been teaching others from your own example. Plan if you can!"

As I already mentioned, I have very a strong, happy and calm relationship with my husband. We have been together since 2002 and married since 2010.

After we got married, for several years we were trying to have a baby, but it wasn't successful. So we decided to visit a doctor.

It got complicated. Our love is the most wonderful, strong experience, but our suffering that started from that moment was even stronger. The doctor did the basic analyses, but he directed me to a specialist. Well, she was a very nice lady and a very good doctor, but I had to have an operation. The first obstacle to this, however, was that my heart because of my previous illness was not in the best shape. So I had to have permission from my cardiologist because total anesthesia could be fatal for my heart. I can't compare the amount of fear in that moment to the moments when I was in the basement during the bombing. But I know that I felt the same. I was afraid for my life. But I wanted a baby so much that I was willing to do what was necessary. For I believed that everything was going to be just fine. I just needed to be strong. So before the operation, I decided to take my life in my hands as much as I could.

I asked myself, "What can I do?"

First, I took a list of my goals that I set earlier, and wrote Postponed! Then I took a new notebook and wrote "New goals," which began with FLY SMART criteria! It was March of 2013. I wrote:

1. I have powerful *mental* strength until 01-01-2014.

2. I have satisfying physical *strength* until 01-01-2014.

3. I *have prepared documentation* that I need for the operation, until 04-04-2013.

So, what can I do to get mental strength? First, I did the LHM breathing exercise from Chapter 1 of this book.

- I took a moment for myself, alone in the bedroom listening to nice, calm *music*.

- I found *peace* in myself and felt my *breathing* and *heartbeat*.

- I asked myself: "How are you?"

- I found out that I was afraid and I needed *help* and *support*.

Then I explained to my husband how afraid I was and that I needed support. He was very kind to me. I didn't have to think about everyday activities (paying bills, buying groceries), he did that for us. He didn't talk about problems; we were just pretending that we are *happy*.

At, the same time, Oprah and Deepak Chopra were organizing a 21 days meditation challenge. I meditated with them every day. I stopped all non-priority activities that were taking time from me. And I went to work every day and gave the best of me, just to stay focus on other things than on the operation. I watched comedies and listened to "happy" music. And I did *the second LHM exercise from Chapter 1 (By now you should be able to "read" from pictures in your mind. Remember this?).*

My physical condition was not good either. So I called my friend who was a world champion in the model fitness category and asked her for help. She made me a fitness and nutrition plan. And I began following it step by step.

- I had cardio training every second day.

- I went to Yoga class once a week.

- I have excluded food with three "white enemies" (sugar, salt and white flour) and everything that isn't organic. Juices were fresh, and food was row. I had three to five meals a day and approximately two liters of water.

- I used tea mixtures, vitamins, minerals, oregano oil...

At the same time, we were all over vetting institutions and finding out what results I would need for the operation. What documentation would I need? We put it on paper, *made a priority list and did it one by one.*

All the results had to be okay, but they were not. I did solve some problems, but others got worse. It was a nonstop circle. But I was persistent and I finally got it! And all the results were okay.

As it was, the operation went well. It was not a serious procedure, though I had been afraid of that fatal anesthesia. Now I know that it was the fear more than anything, but at that time it was hard for me. No matter, everything went well and I got on my feet again. Then we went to the hospital doctor again, and she prescribed injections because I needed them for insemination. She said to me that I couldn't get injections at the hospital because I was not hospitalized. And that I had to go to my local gynecologist to take the first injection at ten o'clock that morning. I did, I went there. But he wasn't working that day and the other gynecologist didn't want to give me the injection because he was not my personal physician. What!? I became angry and felt disappointed and lost.

I stopped again and did our little LHM exercise, and I asked myself: *"What would this problem mean to other people 200 years from now?"* And the answer was *"Nothing!"* So I shifted my awareness back to myself, smiled, and said to myself: *"Solve it!"* Then I went to YouTube and learned how to give the injection to myself.

And I did it that very first time and every day after that. Then the therapy was over, we had to try insemination. It wasn't successful. So I needed the injection therapy again and then a second insemination.

I was lost, but holding on, still doing meditation with Oprah and Deepak, and yoga and fitness. And then, one friend told me to go see a homeopath. I went, and for the first time I told someone about the very difficult childhood I had. My father always had a problem with alcohol. I can't say that he was addict, but he was very violent when he was drunk. It was very difficult surrounding to grow up in. I will not write bad things about him, for he is my father and I forgave him. He has his own battles and demons to deal with. But I needed peace in my soul. And forgiveness is the only right way to achieve peacefulness. I will just say that I was afraid of him all the time when I was a kid. His ego was his leader. But things can't go that way forever. Everything must come to the end, one way or another.

He didn't agree with my going to college, thinking it was a big expense for him. But I knew that I had the right to have a decent life and that college was my way out. I didn't have money, so I needed a National Scholarship. It wouldn't be enough, but my mother promised me that she would help as much as she could, so she got a second job.

I had a lot of knowledge to learn, and I studied day and night. But I passed the exams and earned the National Scholarship. Then I left and took up residence in a new town where I attended college. I sought to finish college as fast as possible so my mother could be released from the second job she took on to help me through college. After college, I got a job of my own and ended up staying in the town where I had gone to college. It became a place I found peace, love and happiness.

So, I found myself talking to a homeopath and telling her about my childhood and family problems and life experiences. And that I thought I might have an obstacle in my mind preventing me from getting pregnant that stemmed from all the fear and problems I had earlier in my life. But I also told her that luckily my father eventually changed and that everything became okay. Or at least I had thought so.

Later that same day and on my way home, I called my mother and told her that I had gone to see a homeopath. But here comes the new challenge! She told me that she was at my uncle's place. At that moment I froze, because I felt that old familiar pain from childhood where something was wrong with my family again. For we were always going to my uncle's place after problems at home.

My mother was very depressed and she was crying all the time. She left our home and my father after extremely big fight. She left with not one single document or one single thing. So, she soon had problems with her personal documents, pension and health insurance. And I was afraid to go obtain her belongings and documents from my father. She needed my help as well with emotional and financial problems. And I didn't have much emotional support to provide, considering the state I was in. Plus, our finances were pretty low because my husband and I had paid so much for my medical treatments. It was a hard time.

Again, I took out a notebook and wrote new FLY SMART goals and priorities:

1. Mother has her first pension on 15-09-2013
2. Mother has new documentation until 01-11-2013
3. My parents are divorced before 01-12-2013

As you can see, these were not my goals, especially not the third one. But, what could I do? She is my mother, I love her and she was "broken." I needed to help her, to solve this crisis and get back to my life. And my husband and I did it. Don't ask how, for it was so difficult and hard. But we made it with the help of our good friends. We all helped her. And peace was again in our hearts and homes. But not for long. For suddenly came a new challenge.

The second insemination wasn't successful. So the doctor told us that we would have to go do in vitro fertilization. And we got a list of needed results for the procedure. Again, I did everything I already had done as preparation for the operation. I also went to the homeopath, received new therapy, and went to fitness and yoga center and continued meditation with Oprah and Deepak. And I made it; all of my results were okay. But my husband's results were not. We needed to concentrate on that side, especially since because the time limit for my results were passing. Here we go, all over again. I said to myself! It was painful. But I knew that pain was not a point of depression or failure, but a point of strength and endurance. And this was the mindset and attitude I adopted and maintained.

As you can see, I haven't made associations for these events. For I really don't want to remember them. Sometimes it is just better to forget. Actually oblivion is one of the greater things in life. Thanks to it we can forget certain things that essentially should be forgotten and then be able to cure our soul.

So I decided to leave all of this behind me and to start over as if nothing bad ever happened. Thus now is the current situation and I am holding a new notebook wherein I am going to put new goals. The truth be told, there are things in life that can't be controlled, that happen no matter what we believe, what we want or what we do. Life is unpredictable and it put up obstacles which we have to pass and conquer. There are things I can't change or influence. But I can change my point of view! I can make any and every situation better and easier! I can be positive! I can expect the best!

The most important thing is to never give up!

This is my personal life. I don't have to write about it, especially because it is a painful experience. But I lived it. So I wrote it. Because I want to show you from my own experience that all you will read in this book is working. Really working! Formulas and algorithms from this book are not only helpful. But they shift awareness. With such help, I was able to move on. And that is why I want to share it with you. As you can see, I don't quit. I am more positive and happier despite all the pain I've known. Though every obstacle becomes a lesson, I am now stronger than ever. I believe. I can. So I must. And I love myself, and more and more. Just as I love every single creature on Earth.

I saw my parent's mistakes and realized that it was because of not enough EQ level, which can lead to a deeper level of misunderstandings. No one is born bad or with bad intentions. People become bad because of millions of factors around them, and those factors make changes in them. But I have forgiven them, both my parents, for whatever I felt I needed to forgive them for.

I am thankful to my mother because she stood by me and my brother's side and she never gave up. I learned from her how to be kind and how to grow up and wonder while a child even through very difficult times. But I also learned what she didn't learn: that I had to love and respect myself as I am and not give so much of myself to other people who don't deserve it. I am also grateful to my father, because I learned that it is not good to let the ego rule one's life. Because eventually you will end up alone and disappointed. I strongly believe that we don't choose our parents but are born to particular families because we must learn the most important lessons from our parents, lessons that are crucial for development of our unique souls. So, don't judge them or anyone else. All of us do as best as we are capable to. All of us have our own battles to wage and demons to conquer.

Find out what do you have to learn from situations that are happening to you over and over again. And the moment you realize it, learn it and practice it, then the negativity will all pass and you will let the pain go. Like it passed in my life. Like I let it go. Believe me. Allow yourself to live in peace and happiness.

Because of all those scars in my soul, I am stronger and I don't let unimportant things or people to impact my life negatively. I believe in keeping company with clean souls and good people!

My aim with Live from Your Heart and Mind is to open new doors for all people, so they can see that things can be different and much better and much less painful. If they seek solutions in themselves, elevate their EQ level, consciousness and soul-self, it can then happen. If they curb or eliminate the ego-self, let go of what is wrong, work to attract what is good, it can then happen. There is no need for anger, violence or aggression. Life is intended for joy and happiness. And it should to be for us, not against us. Why aggression, violence, war and corruption when it all leads to misery and death? Let us make this world a better place. Life desires to be good to us; we have to want to be good to it. For it's true, *"All we need is love."* But love from ourselves to ourselves is as crucial.

Now that we're at the end of this chapter, I'd like to share a special bit of personal information. Our first in vitro fertilization attempt wasn't successful, nor was the second one. We felt emotionally and almost completely broken, but we didn't give up. So we began preparations for the third attempt when my blood test results came in and showed that I was pregnant. Can you imagine our happiness and joy! Thus we expect our baby boy at the end of November 2016. Yes! We defeated the problem with sterility! So I wish to express to everyone who may experience the same problem we did, to believe, have faith, stay strong and maintain the will to solve it. I send all of you a lot of positive energy and love!

Now, I have a special gift for you: ***THE LHM OVERCOMING OBSTACLE ALGORITHM!***

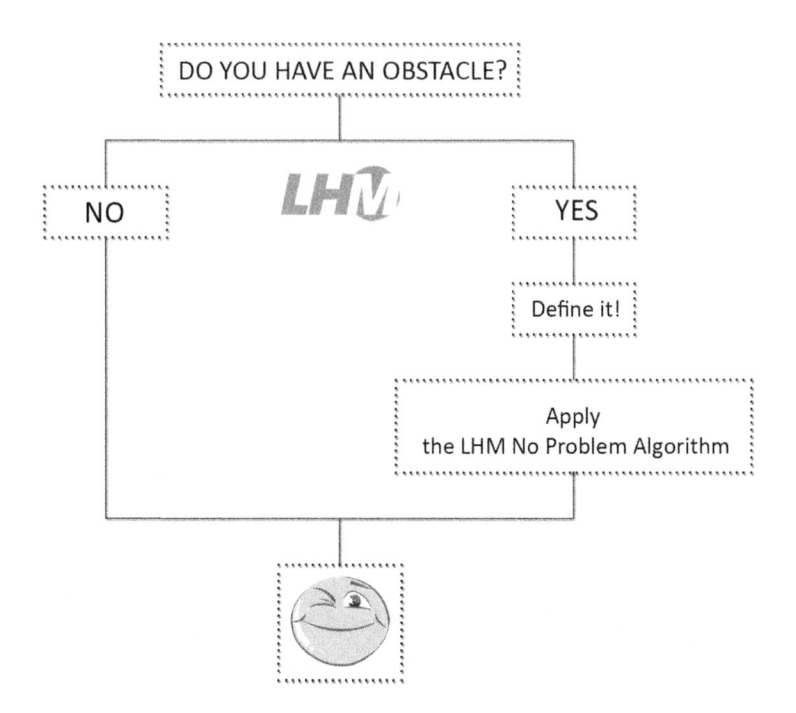

```
            DO YOU HAVE AN OBSTACLE?
                      │
         ┌────────────┴────────────┐
         │         LHM             │
        NO                        YES
                                   │
                               Define it!
                                   │
                          Apply
                   the LHM No Problem Algorithm
                                   │
         └────────────┬────────────┘
                     😉
```

Exercise: If you have any, write your obstacle(s).

1. ....

2. ....

3. ....

Set up an activity plan for every obstacle (translate obstacles into LHM FLY SMART goals).

1. ....

2. ....

3. ....

Exercise: Make your own association drawings for the ***LHM OVERCOMING OBSTACLE ALGORITHM.***

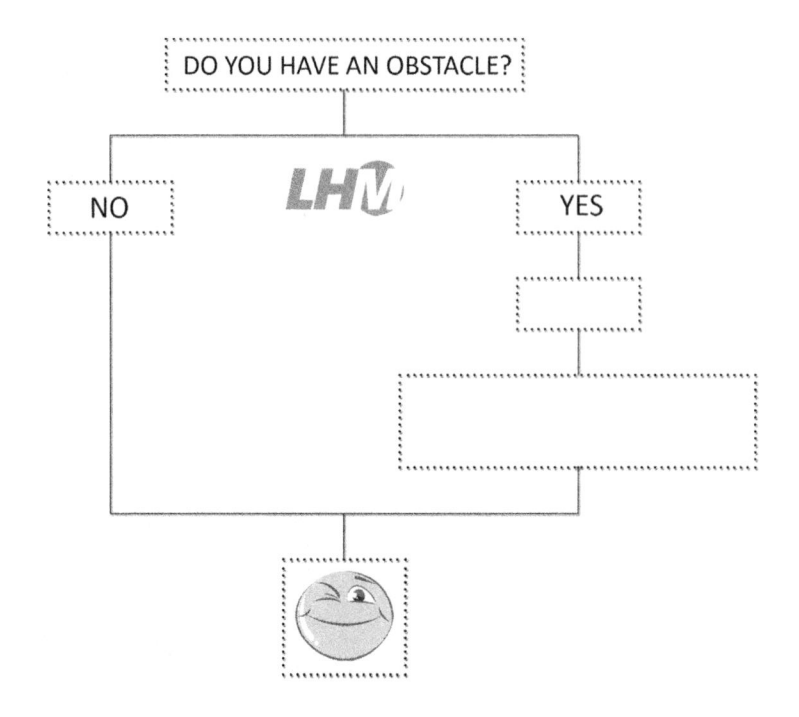

Apply LHM Happiness Formula every day and act to accomplish your goals in order to get over obstacles.

4. LHM IQ Training Question: What is common to the Guinness Book of World Records and actress Sophie Nélisse?

. . . .

CHAPTER 5

LOVE

"You can search throughout the entire universe for someone who is more deserving of your love and affection than you are yourself, and that person is not to be found anywhere. You yourself, as much as anybody in the entire universe deserve your love and affection."

~ Buddha

Commitment, acceptance, understanding, tolerance, trust, friendship, affection, excitement, passion and safety, with a slight shiver and care, make the sense of bliss--that feeling which we call love.

Love is the eternal mystery of life.

Everyone felt love or at some time has thought so, whether it was for that special other person, friends, family, the sea, beautiful sunsets or nature itself. The feeling is extremely complex, so complex that each one of us experiences it in a different way. But whatever that way is, love is that wonderful feeling of joy and satisfaction, the state that takes us on the road *"where dreams come true."*

Love is pure and unconditional. It is a state of your ***soul-self***. If expectations exist in relationships that is not love, then it is ***ego-self*** who wants to be satisfied.

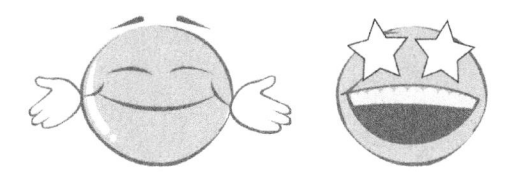

If you are not happy in love, first make sure that it is really soul-self love.

If it is soul-self love and you are still unhappy, be sure that you are not giving it to a wrong person. If he/she does not respect you, your time, your needs or makes you feel humiliated, unloved or even depressed, then these are not your uncompleted expectations. You have the right to feel respected, loved and needed. He/she is not right for you when this is not so.

And if it isn't soul-self love and you are still unhappy, the Universe is telling you that your purpose is to feel soul-self love without any expectations and to ask yourself what is the real reason you are in that relationship. That reason needs a cure. It needs to be solved in some other way, so that you can be on your way to transform yourself into a happy, lovable person and attract the one that deserves you and loves you just as you are.

Often in masterpieces of art, love is described as sadness. But we have to know that **sadness doesn't exist because of love.** Sadness exists because of feeling that we don't have who or what we think we love, and the truth is **that is our ego again.** You must let your soul free and release it from ego.

Sadness also comes from nostalgia, loneliness or disappointment. But must it be so? No!

Being in love is not love! Being in love is passion, and the passion is ego again.

Love is a state of heart and mind!

You choose to be in love the same way you choose to be happy, as we learned earlier, no matter how impossible this might sound now. There are civilizations that don't recognize *"being in love"* or *"romantic love,"* as these are demonstrated to us in romantic literature, according to psychotherapist Zoran Milivojevic. Feeling love is a deeper and stronger healthy state; in fact, the most important state in our lives. Please, try to understand the difference between *"being in love"* and *"feeling love."*

No matter how much I love that particular person, the absolute truth is that the only person who will spend a lifetime with me for sure is the person who lives in me. And that person is me!

You are the only person who will absolutely for sure spend lifetime with you.

You choose if it is going to be your soul-self or your ego-self and if you are going to love and be happy or in love and probably, disappointed and unhappy, at the end.

This is something that must exist in your mind. This is something that you must understand. ***You are never alone, you always have yourself.***

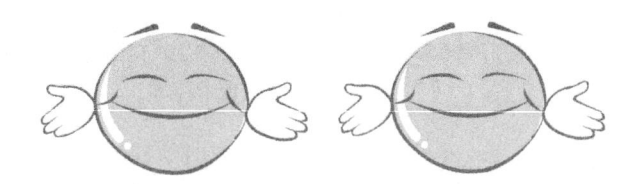

The only thing that is really important is to get to know yourself, your thoughts, your desires and your true self and just be that unique You that you are. Of course, not narcissistic, not egoistical and not your *"Great I am self,"* but your natural self as a person. And if you don't like something about yourself, then change it. But change it for yourself!

It is not hard to tell yourself:

> *"You're not alone"*

"I love you."

"Thank you for being here."

"Don't worry, I'm with you."

Small sentences like this will do a miracle for our consciousness and self-confidence. We will be fresher, more positive and dearer to our self and everyone around us. We will begin to emit positive energy, and positive energy will attract positive people, positive events and positive actions.

We'll see life through different eyes. And most importantly, we will open the door of our *"Inner Me"* and let the law of attraction act on positive signals in order to achieve our desires.

In this fast materialistic time, it is difficult to find yourself, it is difficult to fly into your soul. But if we find just a little time, we will feel peace. Peace for which we strive that lies within us, although we don't even notice it. People usually pay attention to the love they have for other people. Yes, it is one of the most important kinds of love. But if we don't love and respect ourself, people will not love us and we will not be respected by other people, especially by that one particular person. Often, it's just a passion which is equated with love. But passion isn't love. Passion is an aboriginal subsistence necessity of people, like the need to belong, the need for security and the need for sex. Yes, all of this is within the content of love, but much more important is attention, affection, peace and belief in another person.

The most beautiful love is love for family and friends. It is wonderful feeling when you know that at any time you can call someone to be with you, to cheer you up, to help you or just make you smile. That is a sublime feeling of friendship love. Friendship love at first represents safety, attention, confidence and all those beautiful feelings that we call True Love. Friends always remain in our hearts and they are never forgotten or they stay with us if we are lucky.

Choose your friends wisely. You can't live a positive life if you are surrounded with negative people. So choose and accept people as they are. And make it possible to love unconditionally.

Love is the foundation of a healthy family. Families without love are not successful, and in those families all suffer. Parents suffer because they don't feel love for each other, children because they feel like they are not loved. Often these children in their future families create the same pattern. The only natural "clean" love is the love of a parent for a child, and a child for a parent and siblings. It is natural love, a love that does not arise and then disappear, but always is.

Love your family, no matter who they are. You didn't choose them and you are not born in that particular family by accident. You are born because you have to learn what is the best in your mother and what is the best in your father and to become the best version of them and the best, unique version of yourself. Until you find out and learn that, you will feel discomfort and you will be unsatisfied; or even worst: you will feel like you don't belong with them and sadness will live in your heart. Overcome it! Be the change you desire and search for!

For all these loves, if they are healthy, one thing is in common: they make us feel wonderful. According to the law of attraction this is exactly the feeling into which everything is born, from which wishes arrive and goals are made.

Love is essential for success!

Some people will say that they experienced only sadness in love. This may be so, and it may be caused by a feeling of unbearable suffering. But did they contribute to this? We have to be critical with ourselves. Talk to your *"Inner Me"* and you will understand why this is happening. You will realize that perhaps for the first time you heard the child inside you and found you didn't love yourself enough. You need to work on this. You need to love yourself because such love is a precondition for success just as love from another person to you. Inner-self love must be fulfilled or the LHM love formula won't work; or it will work but only in accordance with your feelings. And you will experience sadness!

So pay attention! Inner-self love must be soul-self love, too. If it is egocentric or narcissistic it will not bring good to you. It will attract the same kind of love from another person. And you will face problems. Every time when you do something that he/she doesn't like, you will find yourself in a conflict. Every time when he/she does something that you don't like, you will create conflict. So inner-self love as well as love for others must be soul-self, unconditional and kind. Let go of *"I am the best," "I will do as I want," "I know the best,"* and just be yourself and respect yourself. Let other people be who they are, and respect them too.

You can't change another person. It is a waste of time. You don't even have a right to do it. You just can change yourself and your reactions to others' behavior, however. That is who you are. Find the best in yourself and in others. Accept yourself just as you are. You are perfect just like this! You are magnificent! You are your own creator. Raise your awareness and balance your decisions between heart and mind.

It doesn't matter what we want, it's what we feel that matters! When you feel good, you will transmit positive energy and positive energy will come back to you. When you feel negative energy, you have to answer to it with smiles and kindness. And your life will change. *"There can be miracles."*

Now, I present you the ***LHM LOVE FORMULA:***

1. Discover soul-self unconditional love without any expectation, free yourself from ego.

- Love is pure and unconditional. It is a state of your soul-self.

- If expectations exist in relationships, that is not love. That is ego-self who wants to be satisfied.

- If you are not happy in love, first make sure that it is really soul-self love.

- If it is soul-self love and you are still unhappy, be sure that you are not giving it to a wrong person.

- If it isn't soul-self love and you are still unhappy, the Universe is telling you that your purpose is to feel soul-self love without any expectations and then ask yourself what is the real reason why are you in that relationship. That reason needs a cure, it needs to be solved in some other way.

2. Being in love is not love! Being in love is passion. Love is a state of heart and mind.

3. You are the only person who will spend your life with you! Love yourself!

4. If you don't love yourself, others won't love you either.

5. Make a connection with yourself (breathing exercise from Chapter 1)

- Find your "Inner Me." Help it if it needs help.

- Find what it is that you love to do. Do it! Be the best in what you love! Make an action plan for it and then do it! It doesn't matter if it is not paying off right away. It will pay off when you become one of the best! So become an expert!

6. Love your family, no matter who they are.

7. Choose your friends wisely.

- You can't live a positive life if you are surrounded with negative people. Accept people as they are. Make it possible to love unconditionally. Let go of those who make you feel bad in any possible way.

8. It does not matter what you want, it's what we feel that matters!

9. Happy, lovely feelings bring positive energy. Positive energy attracts more positive energy and then lead to the *"Road of Success."*

10. Love is a precondition to success! Find love in whomever or whatever you like. But most importantly: find love in you!

11. Inner-self love must be soul-self love, too, without any expectation. If it is egocentric or narcissistic you will attract the same kind of love from another person and you will experience disappointment, conflicts and sadness!

12. Convert wishes and dreams into SMART goals, make an action plan and go to the top!

Now you know the recipe. But before you *"eat the cake,"* make it and bake it first. Make it by yourself. Make it as you like, with chocolate or fruits or cheese, with cream, walnuts or hazelnuts. But be unique and you will feel wonderful!

Now, I have a special gift for you: ***THE LHM LOVE ALGORITHM!***

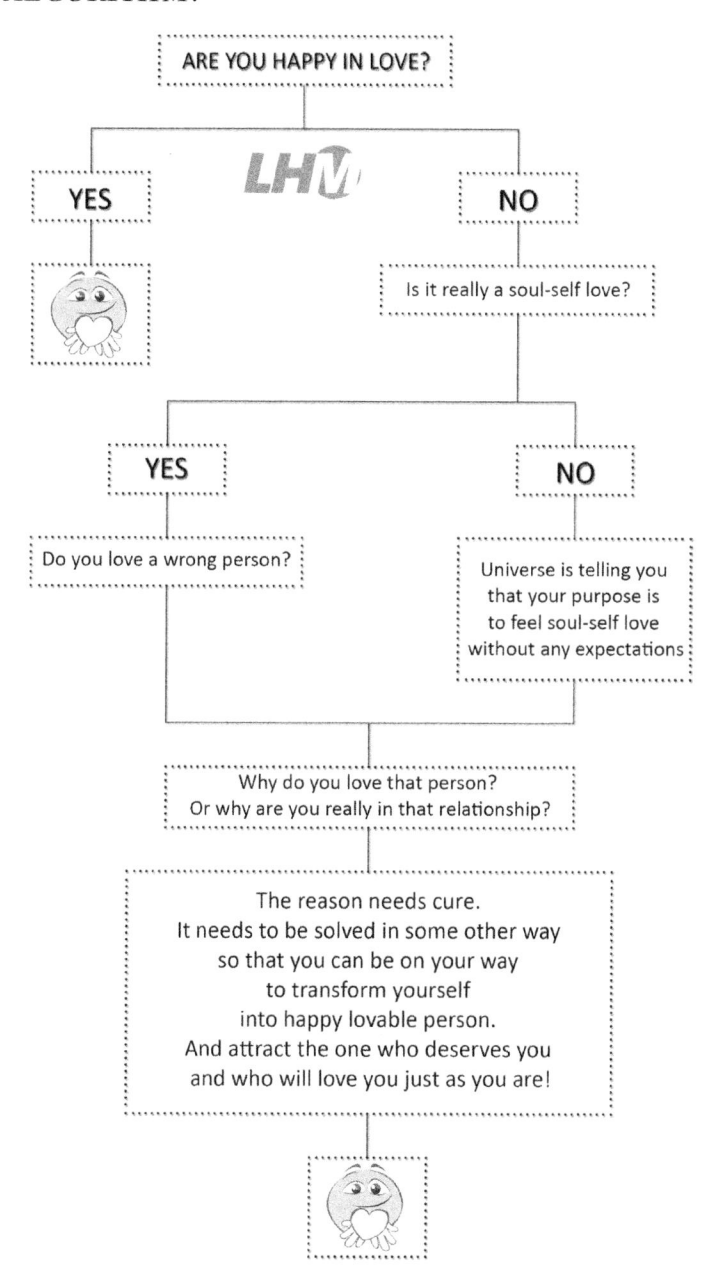

```
                    ARE YOU HAPPY IN LOVE?
                    ┌──────────┴──────────┐
                   YES                    NO
                    │                     │
                  (😊)            Is it really a soul-self love?
                                  ┌──────────┴──────────┐
                                 YES                    NO
                                  │                     │
                        Do you love a wrong person?   Universe is telling you
                                  │                   that your purpose is
                                  │                   to feel soul-self love
                                  │                   without any expectations
                                  │
                        Why do you love that person?
                        Or why are you really in that relationship?
                                  │
                        The reason needs cure.
                        It needs to be solved in some other way
                        so that you can be on your way
                        to transform yourself
                        into happy lovable person.
                        And attract the one who deserves you
                        and who will love you just as you are!
                                  │
                                (😊)
```

Exercise: For every step of the *LHM LOVE FORMULA*, make your own association drawings.

1. ....

   • ....

   • ....

   • ....

   • ....

- ....

2. ....

3. ....

4. ....

5. ....

- ....

- ....

6. ....

7. ....

- ....

8. ....

9. ....

10. ....

11. ....

12. ....

Exercise: Make your own association drawings for the *LHM LOVE ALGORITHM*.

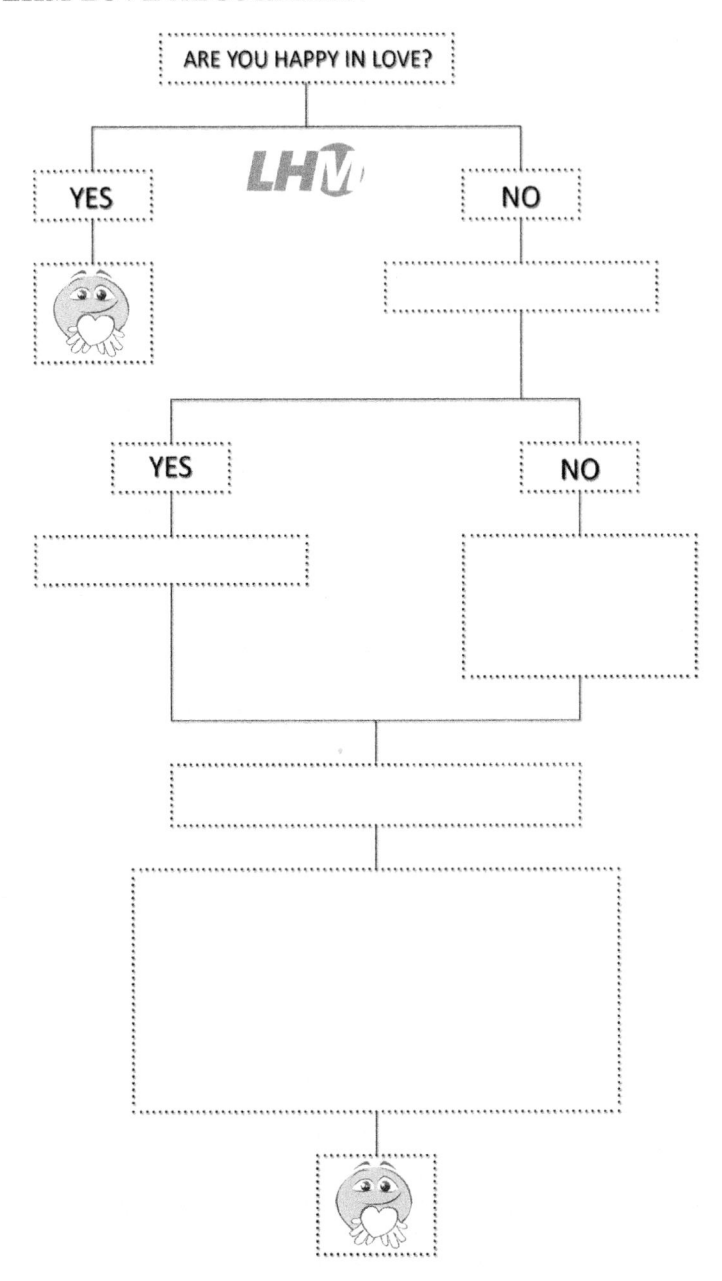

```
            ARE YOU HAPPY IN LOVE?
           ┌──────────┴──────────┐
          YES                    NO
           │                     │
         [ ♥ ]              [         ]
                                 │
                    ┌────────────┴────────────┐
                   YES                        NO
                    │                         │
               [        ]              [             ]
                    │                         │
                    └────────────┬────────────┘
                         [              ]
                                 │
                    [                           ]
                                 │
                               [ ♥ ]
```

5. LHM IQ Training Question: What is the connection between Nikola Tesla and a dentist?

. . . .

CHAPTER 6

SADNESS

"The word 'happiness' would lose its meaning if it were not balanced by sadness."

~ Carl Jung

Sadness and happiness are integral parts of life.

Sadness is like a mirror image of happiness. As well as you can decide to be happy, you can decide not to be sad. But it is much more difficult to make it a real state of your soul, especially when the soul is injured.

Happiness is a state of mind. Sadness is a state of injured soul.

Why are the most exciting, the most beautiful master-pieces in world literature, painting and music created in moments of melancholy, if not sorrow, by artists? But are rarely created during moments of happiness and satisfaction?

When we are happy we forget everything else. We are enjoying happiness and we feel like we have "wings" to fly. All good feelings go to our "outer world" expressed in a smile and our happy behavior. But we forget to transform them into any shape or form of art or work.

When we are sad there is a strong vivid inspiration that leads and needs to become written word, a painting or musical melody, etc. Wide varieties of feelings are bursting to make us feel bad. We aren't smiling. We aren't happy. These feelings make an imbalance between our wishes and reality. These feelings "play the symphony" which attracts more and more bad feelings. They spread all over and want to burst out from our mind and soul. So, they usually burst forth as some kind of behavior or as a work of art.

Does it have to be so? Or does grief actually exist to evoke an inner glow? Can we shine from inside even when we are sad? **Can we convert sadness into happiness?**

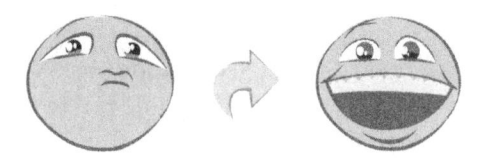

We can! Yes, we can! It isn't easy, but we can! And soon, you will learn how. Stay with me, please.

Your heart and mind are the essence of your existence. They are who you are.

However, sometimes, or even often, the heart and mind "think" differently. The heart wants one thing. The mind wants another. This makes destruction in the soul, a destruction that creates two sides. Those sides need to be joined again.

A man grieves over the unreached, what is lost or even over love. But it is not necessary if we believe that the sadness can be turned into the greatest and purest happiness. Happiness is always in us, but it isn't always recognized.

Some say, *"Time is a cure."* However, we don't forget easily, and time by itself cannot do anything. It can't take away the pain. So, is it time or our hearts and minds that can cure our souls from pain?

The heart feels. The mind remembers and forgets. Time is just a spice needed for new feelings, new memories and oblivion.

So, does time ease the pain or does your mind simply forget? Well, your mind forgets! As you can see, all depends on you! For your mind will do it for you if you allow it.

You will not forget just because you want to. But if you truly want to forget, then first you must forgive in order to reach a place of peace in your soul. You need to forgive yourself and everyone else who hurt you. Who are they? Only your heart knows the truth. Find it out with the LHM breathing exercise from Chapter 1. Ask yourself: *"Who hurt me?" "Why do I feel pain?" "Did I let them hurt me?"* And then learn how to forgive yourself and them. Find your peace. You deserve it! It is the only way and the only state from which you can reach happiness and success at the same time. Believe me. I had such experiences as you already know. And I feel wonderful now, when I forgave and every time I forgive! So, will you!

Does your mind control your heart? Is there a concrete recipe for how to turn sadness into happiness? Is the magic necessary?

Yes, yes and yes! But all the magic you need is in you!

If you love yourself enough, your heart will feel love. Love will send signals to your mind and the mind will activate the oblivion for things that you want to forget. You will begin to see with "different" eyes. You will learn from each painful experience and you will protect yourself with forgetting.

Oblivion is one of the best things that Mother Nature intended for us! Consider what would happen if you were unable to forget, if you remembered everything. Especially if you don't forget situations or events that caused very bad feelings and extreme pain. You would be under stress all the time! Your body might transform all that stress into some kind of illness! So you need to train oblivion, as an emotional and mind process. And also train in remembering, as a mostly mind process. You need to let go of bad feelings and to embrace new good ones. And you will do this only if you don't invoke painful memories and invoke only good ones all the time.

With LHM, you train your emotional side by using the LHM breathing exercise for various questions and by using LHM formulas as well as LHM algorithms. And you train your intellectual side by drawing associative pictures and answering LHM IQ training questions. This is my answer to the question, *"How to do that?"*

However, sometimes we don't even realize that we want to feel sad. Because it is easier than to fight it. But then we don't even realize that fighting is not required. It takes the mind to focus on the positive side and to find something good in everything that happened, although that sometimes seems impossible. Even when we lose someone we love, he or she remains to live on within our memories. But by loving ourselves we will smile upon each and every memory of that person, remembering beautiful moments and say: *"Thank you, God, for giving me the opportunity to meet and love such a great person."* Then, smile. Even if it hurts, smile for that memory. Be grateful for all good moments, and pray to God to take good care of the loved ones who are still alive and present in your life.

Sometimes people are sad because they didn't achieve what they intended to.

If you didn't achieve something you wanted, then set a new FLY SMART goal and move toward it. None of the great minds ever managed to achieve everything on the first attempt. It more often took numerous attempts— maybe even a thousand before success was obtained!

Sometimes people are sad because they feel that they lost something or someone.

Some say, *"Who gives much, loses much."* And what if it isn't a loss, but a form of generosity? What if you introduce it to yourself as your own greatness? As you can see, everything depends upon your perception.

If you were in a relationship where someone left you, you may feel that you gave a lot and got very little or nothing in return. So what? You are great because you gave, even more great if you gave with love, and the greatest you will be when you forgive!

You are probably wondering: *"How can I forgive someone who hurt me?"* Maybe you can't at that particular moment, but if you want it enough you will! Not for that other person, but for you. You will find peace in your soul from forgiveness and you will feel like everything is in the right place. Just give it some time. If you train your mind more, less time you will need for oblivion. And you will almost never forget what is stored on the right side of your brain. Be aware of this. And be your own mind programmer. No matter how hard it may sound, it is easy! Just believe and train with LHM until it becomes your everyday activity and a habit to do.

You are the artwork of your life! You create your own path! You write the "symphony" of your life!

For someone sees all from above. We are not here to judge, attack or revenge. Those actions will only bring pain to our souls and will attract exactly the same actions from others to be brought into our lives. We are here to find peace in our souls. We are here to let other people choose their ways. And for us to choose our own. We are here to learn how to become love.

To smile is a powerful remedy even when we are not happy.

Now, I present you the ***LHM FORMULA for CONVERTING SADNESS INTO HAPPINESS***:

1. Train your emotional side with the LHM breathing exercise, LHM formulas and LHM algorithms.

2. Train your intellectual side with LHM association drawings and LHM IQ training questions.

3. The magic is in you!

4. Love, no matter if you are sad or happy!

5. Love the one who makes you happy and even those who hurt you. If they have a necessity to hurt someone, they need love the most.

6. Love, because sending a frequency of love, you will get love in return. By sending a frequency of sadness, grief will return to you. It is not easy, but it is possible!

7. Take a shower and sing a song you love!

8. Call your friends and go party!

9. Go to fitness training! Play baseball, golf, basketball or whatever sport you love!

10. Do charity work, help someone who needs help!

Remember: It is all your choice! For I encourage you to make your own choices. If I can do it, you can do it! Of course I feel pain. As well as all human beings. For I have feelings and emotions which can be very uncomfortable and painful. But I don't let them rule over me. I use my heart and mind in conjunction with time to cure and to recover and to convert sadness into happiness. You are now familiar with a lot of my life stories, so you know it wasn't easy. But look at me now! Take your life into your own hands and create it as you desire! I am here to show you a completely different way. And do so with LHM, the way that helped me. That is why I want to share all of it with you!

Believe in yourself, in your sincere actions, and things will soon fit into the right place. For sure! Sometimes it needs time, but it will take place! Everything is reachable and possible!

Now, I have a special gift for you: ***THE LHM ALGORITHM for CONVERTING SADNESS INTO HAPPINESS***:

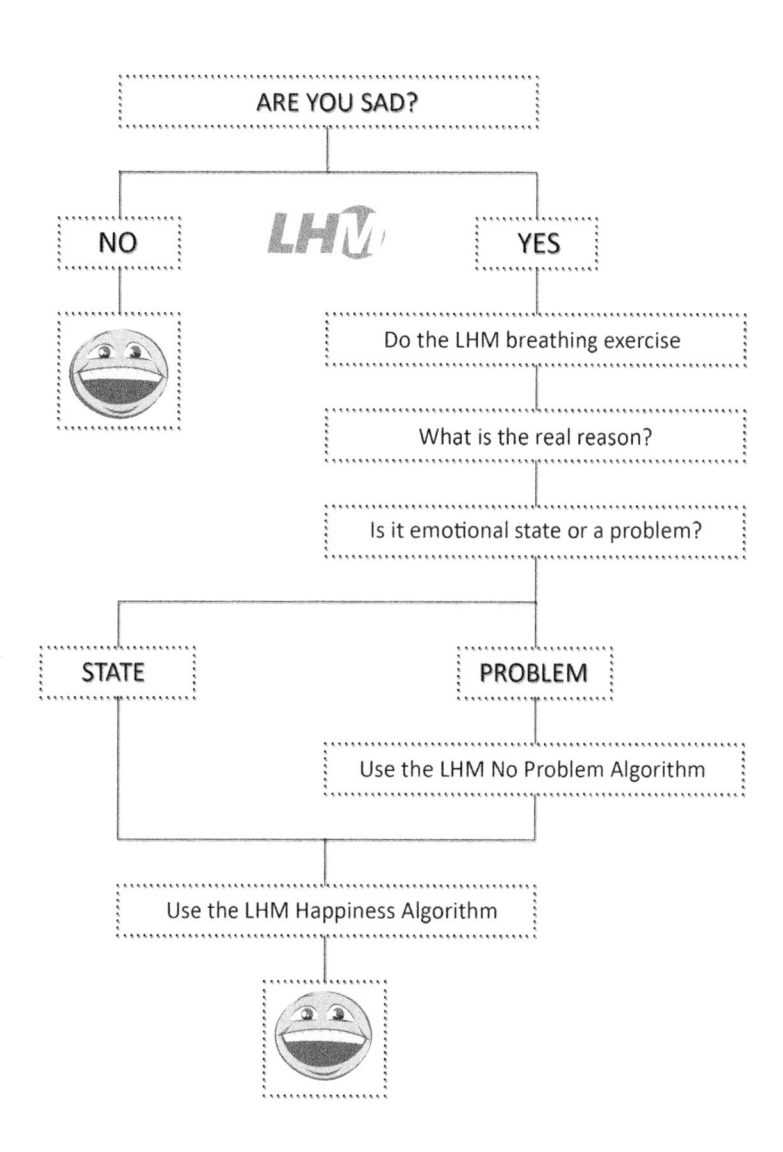

```
                    ARE YOU SAD?
                   /            \
                 NO              YES
                 |                |
                😃        Do the LHM breathing exercise
                                  |
                          What is the real reason?
                                  |
                         Is it emotional state or a problem?
                         /                              \
                      STATE                          PROBLEM
                        |                               |
                        |                  Use the LHM No Problem Algorithm
                        |                               |
                         _____/
                                      |
                          Use the LHM Happiness Algorithm
                                      |
                                     😃
```

Exercise: For meaning of the *LHM FORMULA for CONVERTING SADNESS INTO HAPPINESS*, make your own association drawings.

1. ....

2. ....

3. ....

4. ....

5. ....

6. . . . .

7. . . . .

8. . . . .

9. . . . .

10. . . . .

Exercise: Make your own association drawings for the *LHM ALGORITHM for CONVERTING SADNESS INTO HAPPINESS*

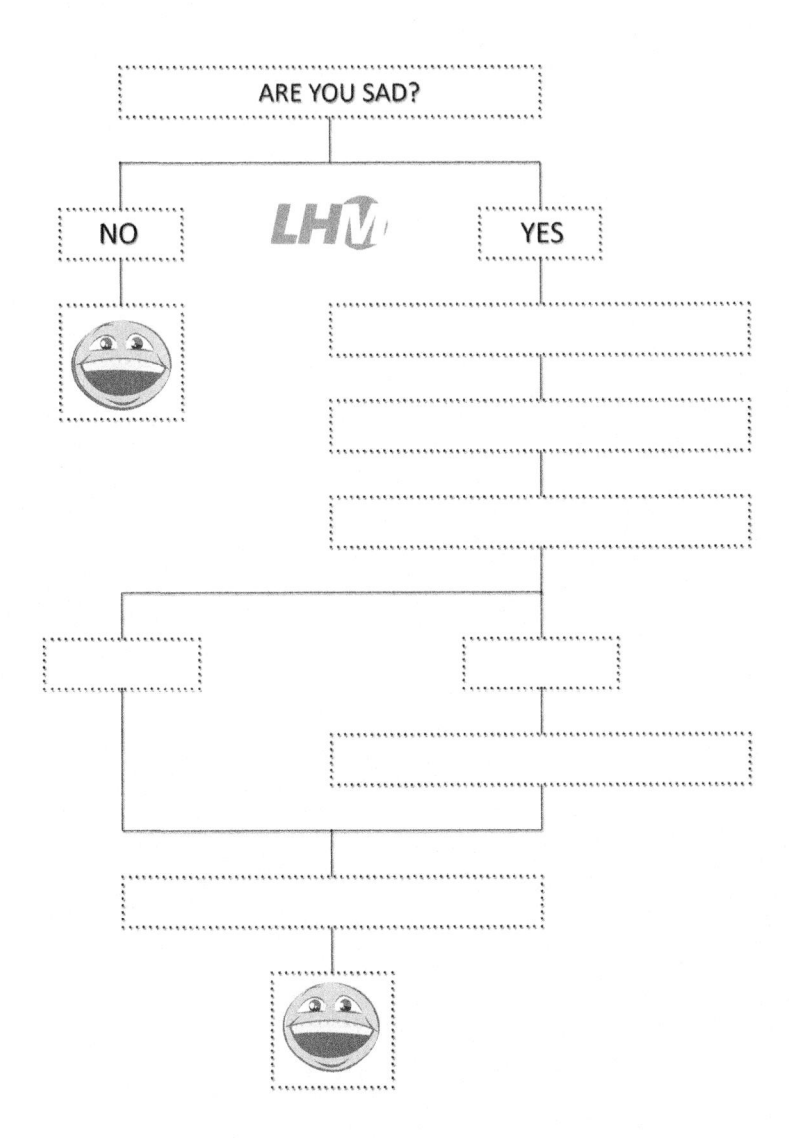

6. LHM IQ Training Question: What is common to a duck and silence?

• •

CHAPTER 7

FRIENDSHIP

*"Don't walk behind me, I may not lead.
Don't walk in front of me, I may not follow.
Just walk beside me and be my friend."*

~ Albert Camus

A lot of people travel through our lives. Some of them go away from us. Some of them remain a short while, and some a little longer and even elicit a smile or tear or two from us, and then go away. And some slowly enter into our lives more deeply, then into our thoughts, our problems and our hearts. And stay forever. All these people, however, with all their emotional states, no matter how long they maintain in our world, leave a trace of themselves to our own emotional state. Some of them are just travelers or visitors. Some become long-time acquaintances and even friends. But only a few become and remain true lifetime friends.

Who is your real, true friend? How can you recognize that his/her heart can or should live inside your own—and do so honestly and truly?

Pay attention to the sparkle in their eyes at every meeting and to the smile on their faces at every encounter. Strive to sense the tenderness in every spoken word and the compassion they sincerely feel for all your pain. Recognize honesty from all your questions. Feel the warm embrace every time you need support. And reflect your look in their eyes when you look at them. Hear your thoughts on their lips when you are silent. See your tears on their faces when you are sad.

Do you have a true friend? Do you have someone who prays for you? Do you have someone who cares for you when no one else cares? Do you have someone who enjoys your happiness? Do you have someone who cries, so that you don't cry? Or are you that someone for someone else?

In both cases, true friendship is a blessing. Whether you give or receive. If you receive, give it back. If you give, you will receive. If not from whom you gave, then from someone else from whom perhaps you never expected it to come!

The richest people are the people who have at least two true friends; and infinitely wealthy people are those who have a few or even many!

In today's materialistic world it can be very hard to find a true friend. Sometimes it is hard to know if it is an honest friendship or it derives from some kind of selfish interest or ulterior motive. Sometimes I think of wonderful people who went through my life and I regret today knowing that they were real friends, but I didn't know it then. Sometimes I think of those people to whom I was true friend and they didn't know it then. But as I now know, so will they know one day. Most of all, I like to think of people who have remained true friends and who have my trust. I keep these persons in my heart forever.

Did a friend ever leave you? Have you ever left a friend? If the answer is yes to either of these questions, then the next question has to be why? What was worth such pain in ending the friendship and forever setting each other apart? What was worth it? Ending such a sincere friendship?

Sometimes we don't understand each other. This is because we all speak our individual languages and our individual personalities get in the way. We all have our own desires and tastes. We all have our own moves and style. And we all have our own defense mechanisms that we use especially when we know that we made mistakes and hurt a friend. Some people use the mechanism of pointing out that a friend is guilty. Deep inside, these people know that it is their fault, though they might not admit it. But often they cannot accept failure, nor admit they are losers. For there are other things they lose in addition to their friendship with you. They can only hope to become winners again, though often it is too late to recapture or resume the friendship they ended with you.

Once, I become an ex-friend in this way. Dear reader, you may judge by yourself, but it is better to learn this lesson from someone who has had the experience, and thus save yourself from all the pain: If something is bothering you, tell your friend in an assertive way. If it happens again, then point it out again, but no more after that. No matter how much you want to save that friendship, no matter how hard you try, if he/she keeps doing what is bothering you and is wrong, then you have to be your own best friend and let go of that friendship. Of course, you have to know when to let go. And it must be before he/she should point the guilty finger at you. Even after this, say what you have to say at the end, and don't keep it inside. Negative energy kept inside is harmful and won't do you any good. Remember, though, that this lost friend has become a teacher to you, no doubt sent by The Universe to make you stronger and teach you wisdom!

There is no place for defense mechanisms in friendships. If the friendship is real and sincere, everything can be surpassed. Strong words can be said, especially if someone hurt us, but we can forgive. We will forgive eventually because we want *peace in our soul*. But will we forget? Well, this depends on us. Do we want to forget? Do we want to go back? Or go forward? I chose forward.

I forgave and asked for forgiveness. Maybe not every person can do this immediately. Some need a little more time, some need a little more courage, and some need love.

Let me tell you something more about my friendships. I was not a favorite person of many during my childhood. At first, because I was an overweight girl; so other girls made fun of me. Boys, on the other hand didn't care about that, so I played with boys. We played sports most of the time. This made a huge impact on my personality. I became stronger. I became a fighter.

Later on, I changed my appearance. But still I wasn't a favorite person among kids. Also, I was always afraid of my father. This because I was never sure what his mood might be. So I didn't invite friends to my home, except for my birthday. They didn't like me because of that and I was hiding the reason why I never invited them. So, they didn't invite me, either. My birthday was on the same day as my neighbor's, and one year everyone went to her place. No one came to my party. Not even to congratulate me or at least wish me happy birthday. I needed a friend. I really did, so I believed that whoever introduced himself as my friend I have to accept him or her without qualms. This brought me a lot of pain. For I wanted to be accepted, so I agreed to a lot of things, even when I didn't really want to agree. I was afraid of everything. I couldn't even show my feelings when I received a gift. And I gave gifts unselectively. I had a big collection of dolls and I gave them to neighbors to play with. They even painted the dolls' faces, cut their hear and clothing and ruined the dolls. But I let all this happen in order to have them as friends.

In primary school, after sixth grade, the situation got better. I was recognized as "the smart one," and everyone who needed it, asked me for help. And I would help them. I helped whenever I could. And I felt better. But it cost me later. For I help people under any circumstance and even when they didn't deserve my help. Eventually I got hurt really bad because people started to use me. I did have one special friend from primary school. And he has stayed in my life ever since, as I hope he always will. He even stayed awake for 48 hours with me when my granny died. So I know that he will wake up in the middle of the night and help me if I need him, just as I would do for him.

In high school, my situation became better for a little while, until I had to travel from the village when we left after a lot of family's problems. Not all of them, but some people around me didn't believe that I had to travel now so far to school, this because my home was nearby in town. They thought I was using this as some kind of excuse to get better grades or something. I was sad a lot and alone often. For the situation at my home was tormenting me. I was really suffering, because seven of us were living at my uncle's house and I didn't have a place to study. They were great, and supporting and nice, and I am very grateful for all they had done for me. But it was a very painful experience for a teenager.

But soon, things started to change. I was accepted by the Scientific Centre in Petnica where talented high-intelligent young people go to do scientific work. I had sent my application in for linguistics, despite my language teacher gave me a low grade on a test, and the fact my focus was in the mathematical department in high school. So when I got accepted to attend the Scientific Centre, my life really did begin to change.

When I was in Petnica for the first time, I met around 70 new people who came to different seminars. I was confused. I didn't know why they had picked me, for I was unsure of my abilities. I was very quiet as a person, and even on spare time, I was often crying. But then, my mentors started to work with me. They explained to me that I had a very high IQ and I possessed the power to use it and to make my life better. That was the first time I realized that I could change my life.

I did some tests there, and my self-confidence test had a very low score. But they gave me special attention and followed my work for years because my IQ results were extraordinary. But they didn't give us all our test results, so I didn't really know how high my IQ was. Until I took the MENSA test 10 years later. Then everything fell into place and it became clear to me why they picked me and why they worked so hard to get me out of my shell.

I published my first scientific work when I was seventeen. And a second one—which became extremely successful-- was published the next year. I developed a system you could use to evaluate manipulation in a text which is transcribed from news broadcasts. In other words, you can evaluate if someone was manipulating you, or lying to you, based on linguistical analysis of the transcribed text of his speech. So I was climbing the stairs of success and eventually was invited to go to Petnica more than 10 times a year. I can almost say I was there more than I was at high school. No matter, the director of my high school was very proud on me. So I went to the Centre every time they invited me while succeeding also at being an excellent student in high school. People who I met in Petnica were people who understood me. They were my new friends. For

I was loved and appreciated. And for the first time, I felt I could really make a difference.

So, it is not your fault if they don't like you. It is not your problem. It is theirs. **Be who you are** and you will find people who will know to recognize you and appreciate you and be your friends.

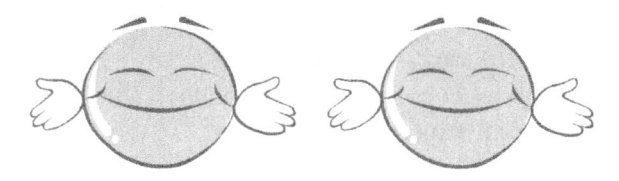

At college it was a completely different situation. I finally could show what I could do. I came to use my own techniques for learning and keeping memory, and I have not fail an exam. Except one time when I quit a test. But there was never an exam I fully took and ever failed. My self-confidence was growing and becoming unstoppable! I loved myself and people started to love me. And during this time I met several great people who, to this day, remain my true friends. Two of them become my godfather and the maid of honor at my wedding.

Very soon I was chosen to be in the 1000 Young Leaders Program with the goal of developing projects that could help revive our national economy which had been destroyed because of the war. There I met a lot of wonderful people who all wanted to help and share their knowledge and support. After that program, I attended a lot of conferences whose aim was to build a peaceful environment between young people from countries which suffered civil war during the 1990s. Our further goal was to establish a vital connection with people from the EU.

I don't mind saying that I became a peacemaker. And I became very good at it because a lot of people from different countries at that time remain my very good friends to this very day – despite the horrors of war that scarred their souls. Not to boast, but a few years ago I was awarded as one of the "Top 30 Under 30 Young Leaders" in the world. Even I didn't expect this! Soon I realized that my greater goal was to become a leader who created leaders, and to be a friend, to help people, to motivate them and share peace, love and happiness. For all this became my initial point for creating this book. Thus my life grew much easier and now consists of many people who support me and are my real friends.

As all of us probably experienced, I was manipulated several times in my life by so-called "friends." Those were business manipulations most of the time. I have studied manipulation in-depth and I know I was double-crossed by many people. No, they were not master manipulators. The mistake was largely mine. I believed and accepted them without reason or clear thinking. And they were bad people.

One point is when I play for a team, I give it my best and my all. And people take advantage of this. For example, the first time a business manipulation occurred was when I wrote my first major project. I had lost about month of my time, and when I asked for a budget specification, I didn't get it. And I suddenly realized all that this particular person in charge wanted was to make money because off me solely for himself. The second time, I wrote a project and they implemented it without even mentioning me or giving me any credit. Then the third time around I came to really believe in an idea, and I gave this project all my time, passion and knowledge. And – you guessed it – I was paid nothing, with everything taken from me and given nothing in return.

So, it finally dawned on me that the problem was me! It was me who needed to change! I realized I had to start respecting myself and not do anything for anyone if I didn't feel right about it. I had to be smart and professional about these things: a contract needed to always be put in place. And if I didn't really want to be involved and didn't know the full parameters and specifics of the project and was given complete cooperation, then it was a project I would not take on.

Okay, despite these manipulations and bad experiences, to this day I still believe there are good people. And I still help wherever and whenever I can, and always will. But I now set boundaries and do business with my head in place and know to be smart in order to save myself from disappointment and lost. And from being manipulated and taken advantage of. This is why I've taken matters into my own hands and have created this book Live from Your Heart and Mind. I want to help people and I feel good about helping them. And everyone who has helped me with LHM will be well-treated, respected and awarded for all they've done. I want them to feel satisfied and good. Because they have become part of something very good and which will make positive change in many, many people's lives.

Treat your friends as you want to be treated is one rule of life I now forever live by. And everyone should.

There are several very good friends in my life who I would like to mention. They are friends who have made a difference and made my life a much better place. They helped me and my family on every field and in every area of our lives. They made it possible for me to work and live in a town that I love and with people I love. They stood by me all this time. I love them more than anything. I know they know who am I talking about, and I would like to thank them now. They – you are like family to me!

As you can see, ***everything comes at the right place at its own time.***

Lessons learned from my experience:

1. If they don't like you as a friend, they don't have to.

2. If they don't like you as a friend, you don't have to like them either.

3. Respect them, even if they don't respect you, be kind and be the better person.

4. You can't help them if they don't want to be helped and they don't ask you for help.

5. If you give your respect, affection and friendly love and it is never enough for them, let them go, they are not your friends.

6. Everything you give to someone else comes back from someone else, although not necessary the same person.

7. Every person in your life is here to give you a lesson after which they leave. It is natural. It hurts but you have to forgive and let them go.

8. When you have to leave. Leave! You will learn your lesson later on. Nothing happens without a reason.

9. Keep in your life just true friends. Don't discard others, respect them and be kind, but remember that they are not your friends.

10. Find out who you really are. Accept and love yourself.

11. Be the best in what you do no matter what they say.

12. Be your own best friend. No one knows you better.

Now, I present you the ***LHM FRIENDSHIP FORMULA:***

1. Be the one who can be trusted, and trust your friends.

2. Be honest, no matter what.

3. Love and show your friendly love.

4. Show respect.

5. Accept all interests, wishes and differences.

6. Accept your friends as they are.

7. Be kind.

8. Be supportive.

9. Be positive and bring positivity.

10. Every time when you are able to, help your friends when they need your help and ask you for it.

Now, I have a special gift for you: ***THE LHM FRIENDSHIP ALGORITHM!***

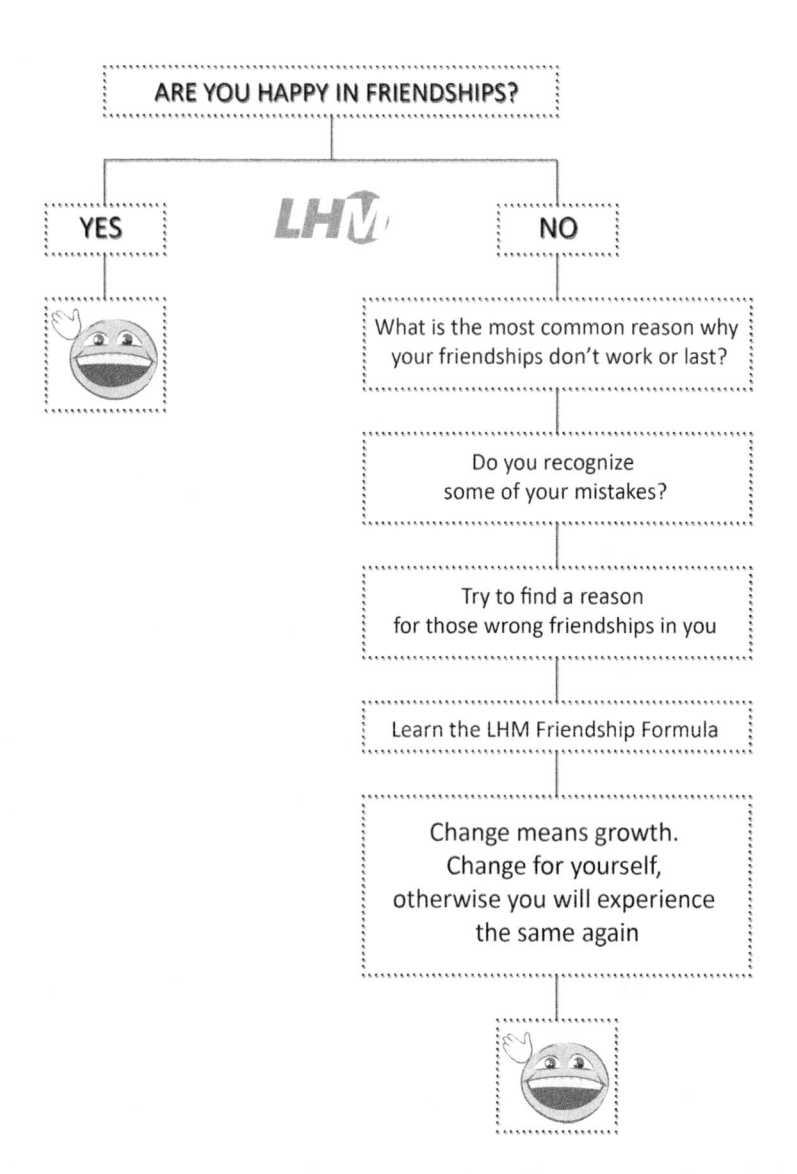

ARE YOU HAPPY IN FRIENDSHIPS?

YES

NO

What is the most common reason why your friendships don't work or last?

Do you recognize some of your mistakes?

Try to find a reason for those wrong friendships in you

Learn the LHM Friendship Formula

Change means growth. Change for yourself, otherwise you will experience the same again

Exercise: For every step of the *LHM FRIENDSHIP FORMULA* make your own association drawings.

1. ....

2. ....

3. ....

4. ....

5. ....

6. ....

7. ....

8. ....

9. ....

10. ....

LIVE FROM YOUR HEART AND MIND 149

Exercise: Make your own association drawings for the ***LHM FRIENDSHIP ALGORITHM***

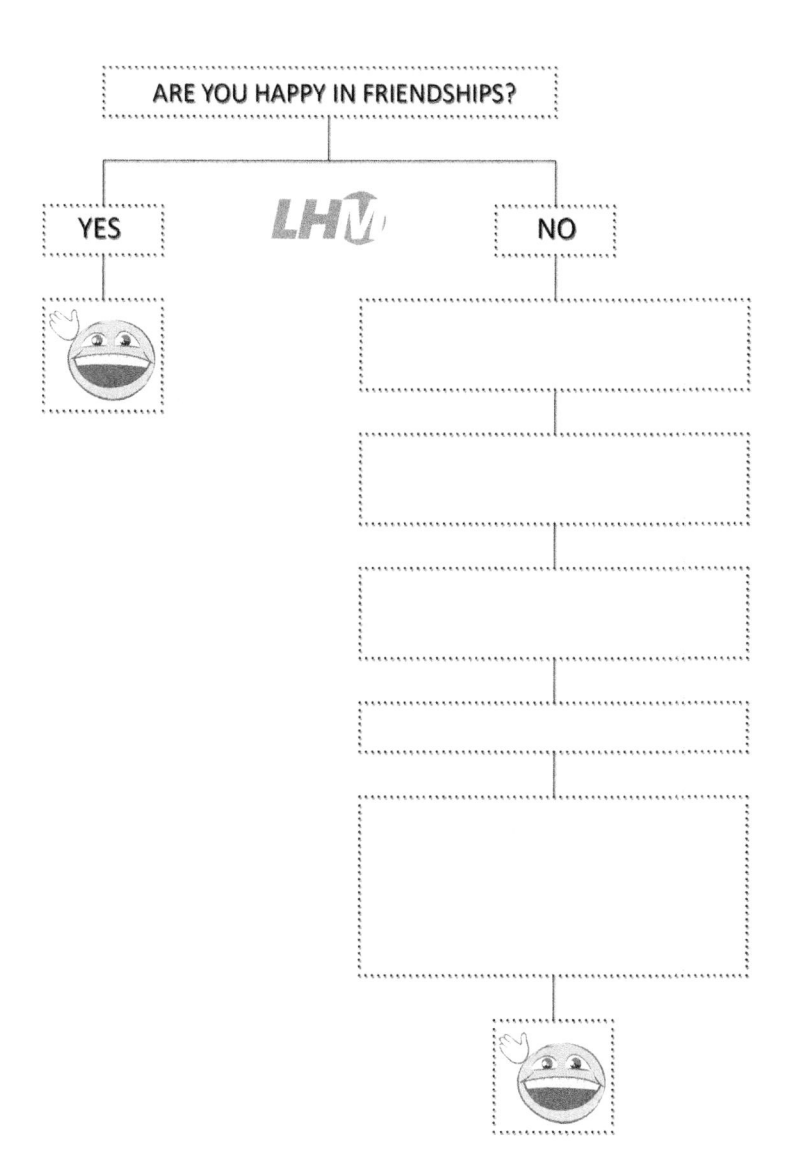

```
          ARE YOU HAPPY IN FRIENDSHIPS?
                      |
        ┌─────────────┴─────────────┐
       YES           LHM            NO
        |                            |
      😄                         ┌───┴───┐
                                 │       │
                                 └───┬───┘
                                     |
                                 ┌───┴───┐
                                 │       │
                                 └───┬───┘
                                     |
                                 ┌───┴───┐
                                 │       │
                                 └───┬───┘
                                     |
                                 ┌───┴───┐
                                 │       │
                                 └───┬───┘
                                     |
                                 ┌───┴───┐
                                 │       │
                                 └───┬───┘
                                     |
                                    😄
```

7. LHM IQ Training Question: What connects the numbers 111.111.111 and 12.345.678.987.654.321?

. . . .

CHAPTER 8

VALUE

"Someone has to die in order that the rest of us should value life more."

~ Virginia Woolf

Is it always necessary to lose someone or something in order to recognize the true value of whom or what we had? Do we realize the true value of people and things in our lives? Can we feel the blessing of life and true happiness if we do not realize the value of what we have and give honest gratitude for it?

That something is meaningful to us, we often realize after we lose or misplace and can't find it. A special, heartbreaking, deep pain we feel only when we lose someone dear to us--someone we love. Life is often unpredictable. But unfortunately, and not uncommonly, people we love do leave our lives, whether we have abandoned them or we are abandoned, whether they continued on their own way or left our world because of death. This pain is different in every situation, but still existent. And it is the pain of loss.

Do we become sad because we lost somebody loved? Or because we suddenly realize that that someone will no longer be with us to love us, laugh with us and hug us – in other words, because we miss them?

Do we only then really remember their smiles, their jokes, the sparkle in their eyes, their tenderness, love and honesty, and the attention they gave to us? Do we only then really remember that we love them and we don't want them to leave us? I mean, is it really necessary that something so dire or tragic to happen to wake us up? Do we need someone to turn his back on us, so that we can come to know his real value? Why only then? Why not earlier? Why not when he or she is with us?

All of us often make mistakes. We take care of someone we love and come to believe that they love us too. And we share a bond and special feeling with them and trust it will always be reciprocated and mutually demonstrated. But we forget to do this. We forget to express our feelings and even come to take people for granted, and they us. Then sometimes the chaos of everyday life comes on stage: school, college, work, obligations and more obligations. Sometimes we disappear in obligations and forget the true value of life. We forget that "it doesn't matter how many times we breathe during a day, but that it is more important how many times we ran out of breath."

We often forget the importance of our loved ones and dedicate ourselves to career success and all kinds of other things. But are things more valuable than people?

Is it more valuable to have a big apartment, a nice car or to feel love with dear people and smell the pine trees and share the snow or sea with them? Is it more valuable to follow certain things or be guided and embraced by love? And so, day after day, nervous about this and that, urgent about material things and slowly losing the thread that connects us, are we disappearing into the fast-moving city of hustle and bustle and becoming slaves to the material needs and desires of our modern lives?

And what about those people who love us? Usually (and unfortunately) they are no longer with us when we finally know to pause for a moment and ask ourselves: What are we doing?

Is it necessary that someone who loves us to stop calling us? So that we might understand that we were selfish, that we should pay attention, and give support and love? Is it necessary that someone leave us because we didn't pay attention? In order to realize that we should have? Is it necessary to discover love and appreciation after it is too late? Why would this have to be so? We have always at least a moment of time, at least before bedtime to express our love and appreciation. We have at least a minute each day to pause and say: "Thank you, God, for this family, for these friends, for these loved ones. Thank you, God, for them and all the blessings in my life." This we can do now and every day and not wait to do after they leave and it is too late. And when we are only left with, "God, please return them to me!" The truth be told, we need to wake up and snap out of it! Before it is too late.

The value of love and appreciation lives in, and can be shown in small signs of attention and affection: in a smile, a wink, a kiss, a hug, in a pat on the back and brief word of praise. This is the way to build our fortune, to allow happiness to open new doors for us, and growth and prosperity to enter our hearts and homes. We need to acknowledge regularly those beside us and in our lives who love us and give our lives value and meaning. Then may our lives become enriched and full of joy – of the kind that is consistent and lifelong! For such dwells in all of us. We just need to pause periodically and take stock of it, to ask for forgiveness, to forgive, to go through life with our pure soul, bright face and heartfelt smile. And share our sunlight with others as they share theirs with us!

Sometimes it is inevitable that we must lose someone we love. But we should never let them leave because of us, unless they chose that as their new way. Then we have to let them go, and we have to say and mean that we wish them happiness. If staying is really worth the value, they will realize it. They will understand and will try to return to us.

All these questions are here to make us realize that something is never worth more than someone, and that people who love us are our most valuable fortune and foremost treasure in life.

We have to wake up and realize that we need to keep who we love and realize the infinite value of others while they are still beside us and with us. This includes accepting differences and tolerating different opinions, interests and tastes. For we are all unique. In all of us there is something magnificent, something that has immeasurable value.

Say to your loved one: "I appreciate you. I'm never going to leave you. I understand your inimitable value and how blessed I am to have you with me. For I thank God that I have you in my life."

The moment you realize all of this is the moment you will be released from your ego and liberated from a great preponderance of potential misery, loneliness, disappointment and pain in life.

Now, I present you the *LHM VALUE FORMULA:*

1. Remember someone you have lost.

2. Did he/she leave you or it was vice versa?

3. Don't blame him/her. Try to find a reason for that lost from inside you. Fight with your ego for it. That reason needs a cure inside of you. You can only change yourself and save yourself from new pain.

4. Remember someone you love, someone who is in your life.

5. Every evening find few minutes to thank God/Universe for him/her.

6. Every now and then find some time to give your complete attention to that person.

7. Show your love in whatever possible way.

8. Have you ever left someone over something?

9. Why did you do that?

10. Was it worth it?

I have a special gift for you: ***THE LHM VALUE ALGORITHM!***

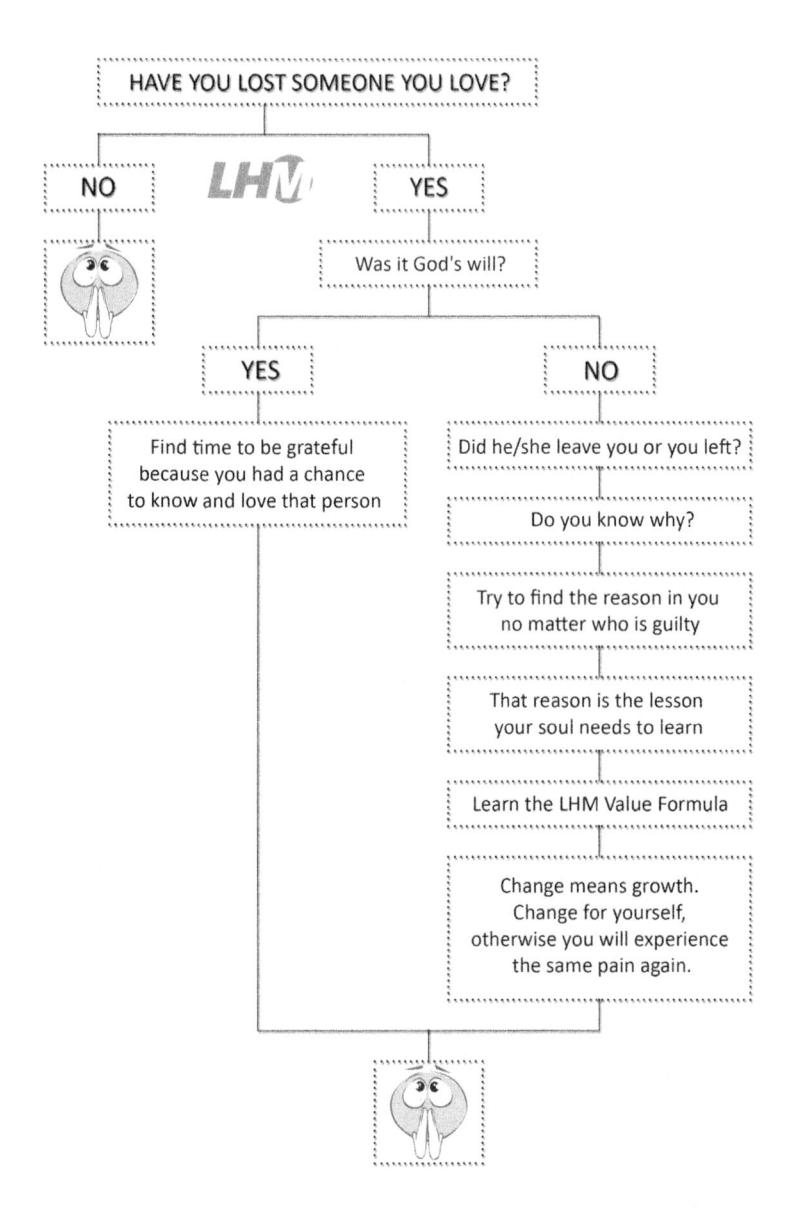

```
                HAVE YOU LOST SOMEONE YOU LOVE?
                    │                      │
              ┌─────┘                      └─────┐
            NO          LHM                    YES
             │                                   │
             ▼                             Was it God's will?
                                                 │
                                    ┌────────────┴────────────┐
                                  YES                          NO
                                    │                           │
                        Find time to be grateful    Did he/she leave you or you left?
                        because you had a chance                │
                        to know and love that person    Do you know why?
                                    │                           │
                                    │                  Try to find the reason in you
                                    │                  no matter who is guilty
                                    │                           │
                                    │                  That reason is the lesson
                                    │                  your soul needs to learn
                                    │                           │
                                    │                  Learn the LHM Value Formula
                                    │                           │
                                    │                  Change means growth.
                                    │                  Change for yourself,
                                    │                  otherwise you will experience
                                    │                  the same pain again.
                                    └────────────┬──────────────┘
                                                 ▼
```

Exercise: If you have those experiences, use the LHM value formula for the person that was left by you, the person that left you and/or the person that you have lost something over. For every step of the ***LHM VALUE FORMULA***, make your own association drawings.

1. ....

2. ....

3. ....

4. ....

5. ....

6. ....

7. ....

8. ....

9. ....

10. ....

LIVE FROM YOUR HEART AND MIND   161

Exercise: Make your own association drawings for the
LHM VALUE ALGORITHM

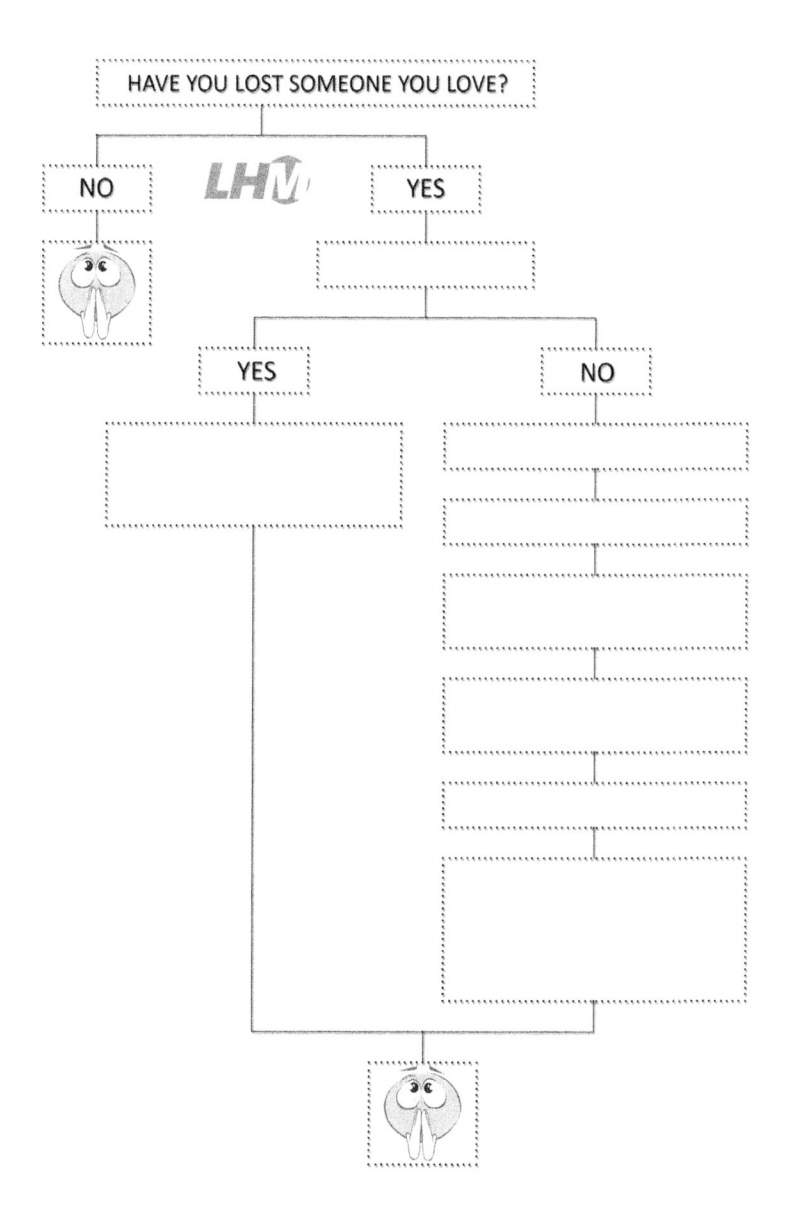

HAVE YOU LOST SOMEONE YOU LOVE?

NO   *LHM*   YES

YES   NO

8. LHM IQ Training Question: What is common to elephants and plants?

. . . .

CHAPTER 9

WORDS AND THOUGHTS

"Think twice before you speak, because your words and influence will plant the seed of either success or failure in the mind of another."

~ Napoleon Hill

The words that we speak can create the world around us. Words that we don't say but reserve within our thoughts can create us. We're not even aware how important it is to carefully choose the words that we speak to other people. But words are often the only way to express our happiness, fear, anxiety, anger, sadness or any other feeling we have. This is especially so if it is a long-distance relationship. Thus *words* are formed from the human need to communicate, to convey our thoughts and to *express our feelings.*

Often, though, we don't think about what we think about. No matter how absurd this may sound, it is important sometimes to stop, interrupt the flow of thoughts and wonder what you are thinking about. Does it matter? Is it nice? Yes, it's nice! Great, then continue to think about that nice thing! Nice thoughts help create a beautiful soul! Is it ugly? Then stop! Don't think more about that ugly thing. Why waste or lose your time over it? Do you want these bad thoughts to attract negative things into your life, to attract sadness? Of course you don't. Why would you want something like that?

Can those ugly thoughts become nice? Yes! You can control your thoughts. You can be the conductor of this orchestra! You simply have to focus on your desires, not on the barriers to those desires. For focus can allow you to control the flow and content of your thoughts and prevent them from wandering off in an uncontrolled direction!

If you already don't behave this way, you have to focus on the beautiful characteristics of people who are around you. And stop denigrating or complaining about their characteristics that don't suit you. Because this way you will only get what you talked about and you will be more and more unsatisfied and in unbalance with your wishes.

Louise L. Hey said that on her road of healing she had to stop gossiping about other people. When she stopped gossiping, she realized that she no longer had anything to talk about. She found that all the years she had focused and spent on gossiping wasted her time in learning or knowing little about anything else! Like a lot of trivia, gossip is so mundane unintellectual, as well as petty and unconstructive. By gossip Louise saw she only emphasized the bad things about other people and thus attracted bad things into her life because of it. From the moment she said, "God bless you. I let you go," she felt she had dropped a huge load off her chest. She felt this sudden freedom and then began speaking beautiful words about everyone. So that when she talked about someone, she talked only about their beautiful qualities.

You see, you are the *Majesty* of your life and possess a lot of beautiful qualities, as well as every one of us does. We just have to let these beautiful qualities become dominant and fill our thoughts. Thus if you don't have anything nice to say, then remain silent and don't think about it and say nothing.

For as all of should know, words can be quite powerful! More powerful than physical weapon, actually. And if used wisely, they can be a powerful force for goodness and positive change! Perhaps more powerful than anything else in the world! There is the popular saying in my country that *"A kind word can open an iron door."* Then of course, one of the most powerful words in every language is the word "love." For love is the thought and the feeling that can be described often with very few words and always in very beautiful words. Combinations of almost any other word in every language cannot match the strength and beauty of love.

Pause for a moment and say these words out loud:

    Life

    Love

    Happiness

    Forgiveness

    Tenderness

    Attention

    Desire

    Value

    Faith

Notice how all these words awake positive side of your thoughts and soul and light up your day. But if you pronounce sadness, pain, loneliness, tears, hatred, rejection or death, each of these words does not have the same effect and do not elicit thoughts or feelings that feel good. So why do we use and speak these negative words? They exist in order to express a situation or feeling or perhaps to communicate a condition when necessary. But don't use them in any other context, especially when you know now that they do not cause or lead to any good.

Unfortunately, when we feel pain in our souls we often do not defend or immerse ourselves with kind words. Some people even attack other people by saying something they don't believe, because at that moment they are trapped within their own bad feelings. This, too, does not bring any good. Try to replace these hard words with kind words. It may be difficult at first to begin this process. It was very difficult for me to initiate. But when I accepted this good purpose and practiced it regularly, I made it happen. Even when suffering any kind of verbal attack, I would respond with kind words. Such people became confused, but these same people never approached or treated me again in such a manner, and I created a positive vibe, that had a positive effect upon them, too.

We must learn to balance our thoughts with our feelings, and our feelings with the words we speak and say.

We need to be careful and don't express our anger or frustration in the wrong way, because we will eventually regret it. Then we will have to ask for forgiveness. For we will want to erase such words. But words are things, and once spoken, can't always be taken back. So, we can only wait and in these cases hope to receive forgiveness. And pray that the person who fell victim to our harsh words will forgive us and not leave our lives forever.

It is actually not so difficult once we start practicing and becoming proficient at controlling our thoughts—which control what comes out of our mouths. We just need to remember that words are things which have impact upon others and that we need to want to always have a positive impact on others. We might also remember that scene from the Bambi cartoon when bunny Thumper declares: *"If you don't have something to say that's nice, better don't say anything at all."*

So let this be the moment when you tell yourself that you will stop thinking about bad things and events, and find something good in every situation. Now is the time you will begin controlling your thoughts and infusing your mind with good and positive thoughts. And when you speak, your words will be words that come from good and positive thoughts. For our intention must always be to do good and not bad, and to speak well and not ill of others.

If you can listen to others who speak lies about you and yet don't say a single word about it, you will show your self-confidence and strength of character. But still, if you need to defend yourself, then by all means do so! But choose your words carefully. For remember, words are things that have impact. But love yourself above all else, and raise yourself above the bad and be above the petty. One thing is certain, there will be bad things we will encounter in our lives. But we do not have to become them or allow them to pervade our thoughts or control our minds. Discard them! Let them be and simply move on. Don't attract more!

Let this be the moment when you stop and be honest with yourself, when you let go of all negative thoughts and invite only good thoughts and feelings into your life.

Soon enough you will find it is not so difficult. In fact, it is an old and well-known philosophy:

> *"What you give, that shall you get."*
> *"What you sow, that shall you reap."*
> *"What you think, you become."*

Think of beautiful things and feel good. Do fine and fine we will be your experience. Learn to control your thoughts and you'll see miracles happen! It worked for me. It will also work for you!

This is one of the most powerful tools that I used in my life, and still use. It helped me in every area of my existence. I am sharing it with you in order to help you too, so that happiness may become your lifestyle.

Now, I present you the *LHM FEEL-THINK-SAY-ATTRACT-LIVE (F.T.S.A.L) FORMULA:*

1. Think about what you feel.

2. Think about what you think about.

3. Think about what you talk about.

4. If these three aspects are not balanced, the Universe will give you bad, chaotic experiences.

5. If you feel good, just do as you do!

6. If you feel bad, stop and ask yourself why (LHM breathing exercise from Chapter 1).

7. When you detect a problem, ask yourself what you think of it and how you talk about it, and with whom?

8. Stop thinking about and talking about bad things!

9. Talk and think only about good things!

10. Feel good. Think about good situations. Speak and think kindness. You will attract the positive and it will become your lifestyle!

Now, I have a special gift for you: ***THE LHM F.T.S.A.L ALGORITHM!***

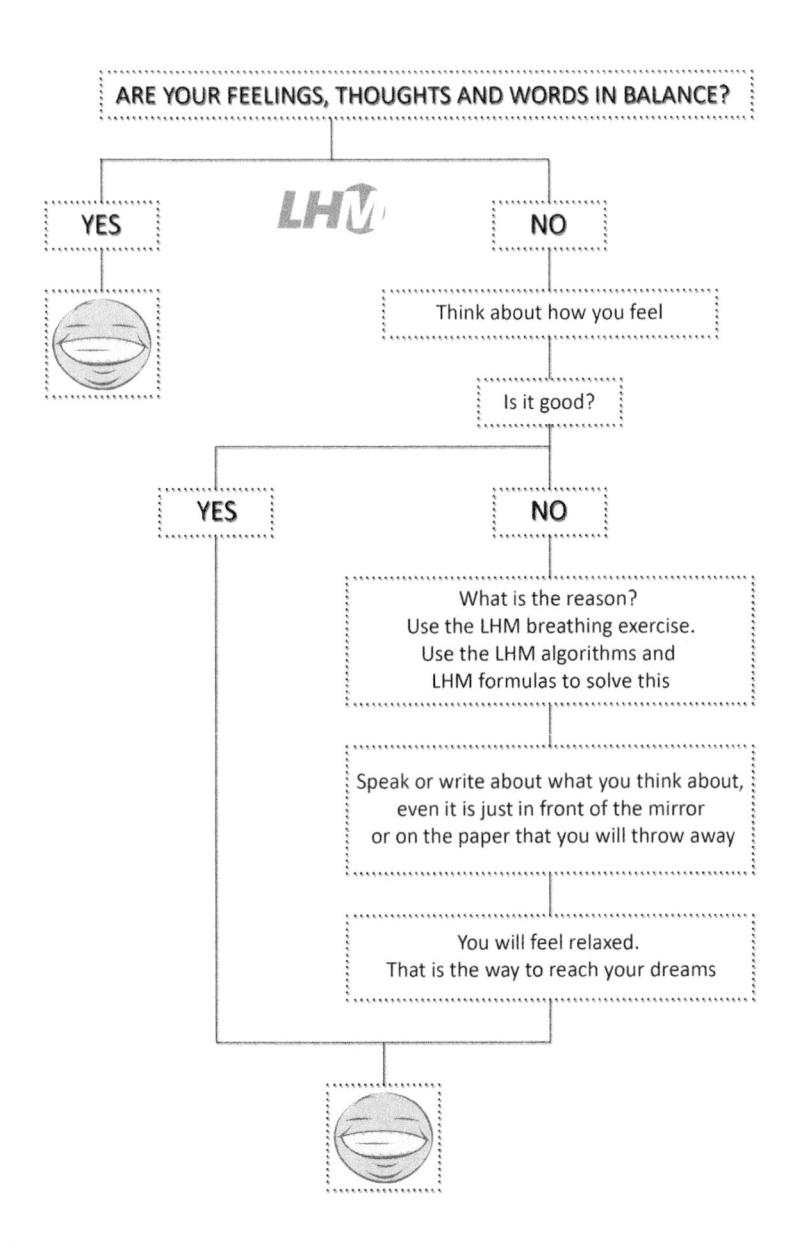

ARE YOUR FEELINGS, THOUGHTS AND WORDS IN BALANCE?

YES

LHM

NO

Think about how you feel

Is it good?

YES

NO

What is the reason?
Use the LHM breathing exercise.
Use the LHM algorithms and
LHM formulas to solve this

Speak or write about what you think about,
even it is just in front of the mirror
or on the paper that you will throw away

You will feel relaxed.
That is the way to reach your dreams

Exercise: For every step of *LHM F.T.S.A.L FORMULA* make your own association drawings.

1. ....

2. ....

3. ....

4. ....

5. ....

6. ....

7. ....

8. ....

9. ....

10. ....

Exercise: make your own association drawings for the
LHM F.T.S.A.L ALGORITHM

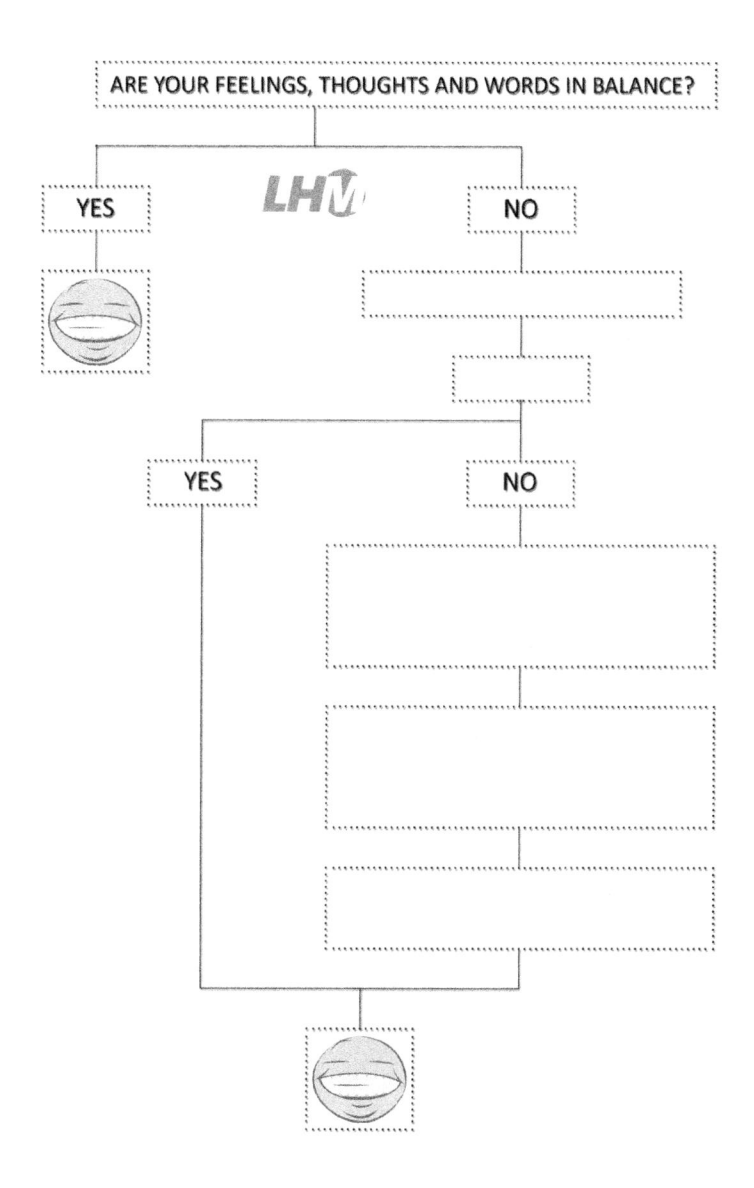

```
ARE YOUR FEELINGS, THOUGHTS AND WORDS IN BALANCE?
         │
   ┌─────┴─────┐
  YES         NO
                │
              ┌─┴─┐
              │   │
            YES   NO
```

9. LHM IQ Training question: What is common to writers Miguel de Cervantes and William Shakespeare?

. . . .

CHAPTER 10

PEACEFULNESS

"To enjoy good health, to bring true happiness to one's family, to bring peace to all, one must first discipline and control one's own mind. If a man can control his mind he can find the way to Enlightenment, and all wisdom and virtue will naturally come to him."

~ Buddha

How do we find our inner peace in this fast-paced world, when almost every day is pushing us to the brink of turmoil?

We are all unique, fabulous creatures, the most developed and the most perfect on our beautiful planet.

But are we aware of this? Very often, led by everyday life, we forget the fact that we are unique and brilliant in our own existence. Only at times, when we separate a few minutes alone in the silence, we listen to our own thoughts. With a deep breath, beautiful music and solitude perhaps, we can find our true self and realize what it is that makes us happy.

Maybe people who have everything are not happy; but those who are grateful for what they have, certainly are.

When you look in the mirror, what do you see? Smiling and satisfied or a sad and unhappy person?

If you're not smiling in the morning when you get up out of bed, if you have a concern on your mind, then you need to work on that feeling, to discover what it is that leads to that imbalance. Can you influence these things, or not?

If you can influence, don't waste your time, make an action plan, jump out of your bed, raise the blinds, let the sunshine in the room, say "Thank you" for everything you have and grab a day! Go and make it happen!

If you cannot influence, then try to calm down, lie down, relax, indulge in a warm bath or meditation, go to the gym, jogging, watch a movie, do some work and try not to let any negative thoughts create your reality. Believe that everything has a reason why it happened. Believe in the best.

It's hard in the beginning. Of course, it is hard. Especially if you don't live alone, because you might not have a good, healthy relationship and someone you can rely on. But is this specific person really the one who brings you the best in life? Is this person here to teach you something, to show you that you can do better and they are someone who is better for you? Someone with whom you will be happy and will teach you how to let go?

No matter how much we want someone, if we are sad with him/her then our emotions indicate us that something is wrong. He/she is not the one. And we have to let go.

We need to be strong. You must find the strength to make it your advantage. It can be hard because you might have kids and family and a busy life and may not have much time for yourself. It is hard because we meet a lot of different people and if we let the wrong ones influence us it will become even harder to find harmony and peace. Maybe some of those people are unhappy individuals. But just remember that they have their own struggles in life and maybe something unknown that seriously affected them to cause their unhappiness and negativity. Remember that it is not personal and you need to let them go.

Maybe some of them are co-workers or acquaintances we hardly know who don't live life the same way that we do, who have no peace in their lives and have to survive amidst constant turmoil and chaos. So let them. Let them live as they find it necessary and appropriate. But meanwhile, we can at least find common ground with them and respect for each other. The adage "Live and let live" is one to take to heart.

Maybe some of them are our friends. And they have a world of their own for themselves. Sometimes we may not understand why they behave in the way they do, but we can't do anything about it. Not really. Or perhaps we can try to point to them some aspect of their behavior that bothers us. But they might not change that behavior because that is who they are and are not open to change. So, again, let them be.

Thus how can we find peace? Consider these ideas:

1. Dedicate yourself to yourself and to your family. Devote yourself to small and beautiful things.

2. Take a job which is something that gives you necessary financial security, and love what you do, and strive for excellence in order to achieve better results and more self-satisfaction.

3. Think about who your real friends are and who donate their time, kindness, heart, support and respect to you. Be dedicated and good to them.

But what if we're disappointed by our friends, then again we will be losing inner peace, right?

Well, that's a risk we accept when we choose our friends. All people are basically born good but sculpted later by family, environment, education and society. Still, even give a "Thank you" to the people who bring you discomfort, because they are your best teachers. They showed you that you should grow and overcome them. Life is nothing but a stream of learning, actually. From each situation we become more mature and more aware, or so at the very least, should. Until the time when each of us finds his or her own inner peace.

Now, I present you the ***LHM PEACEFULNESS FORMULA:***

1. Look in the mirror. What do you see? Are you happy?

2. If you are happy, that is wonderful!

3. If you don't feel happiness, do the breathing exercise from the Chapter 1. Find out what the real problem is.

4. Can you influence a change to it?

5. If you can, then set a FLY SMART goal, make an action plan and do it!

6. If you cannot influence it, try to calm down, lie down, relax, indulge in a warm bath or meditation, go to the gym, watch a movie, do some productive work, but do not let any negative thoughts create your reality!

Now, I have a special gift for you: *THE LHM PEACEFULNESS ALGORITHM!*

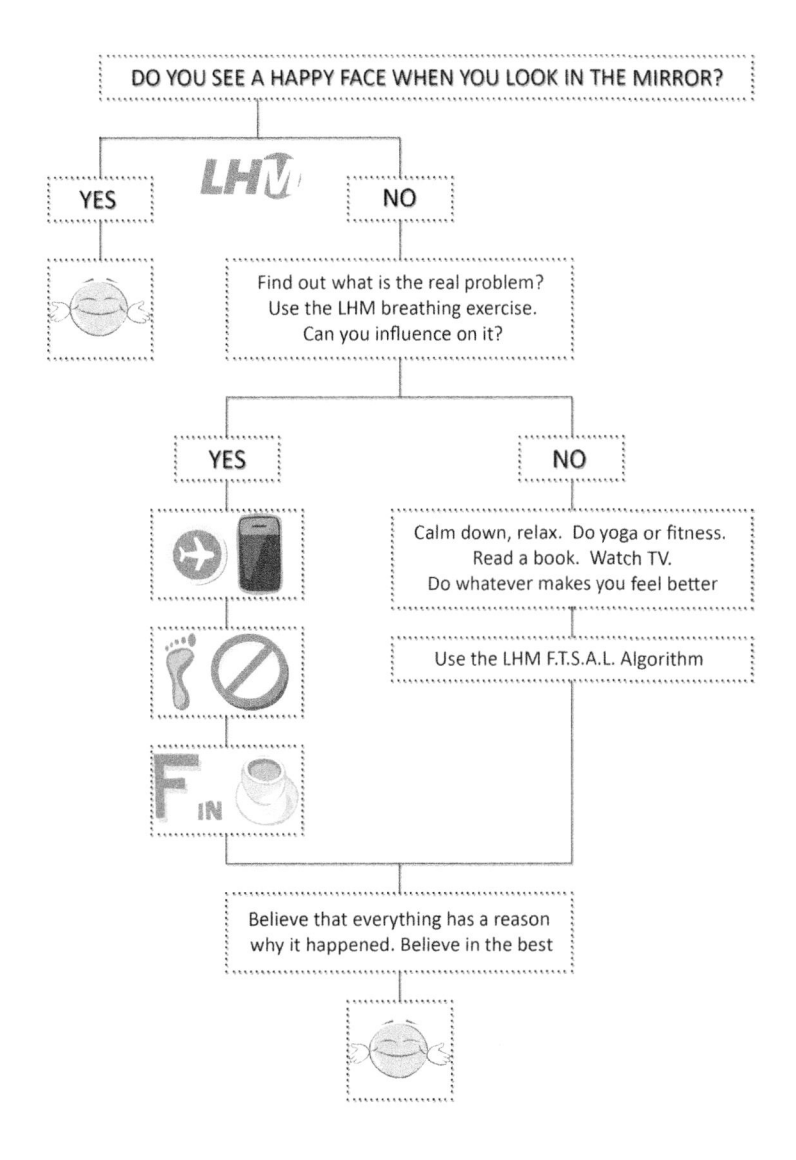

DO YOU SEE A HAPPY FACE WHEN YOU LOOK IN THE MIRROR?

- **YES**
- **NO** → Find out what is the real problem? Use the LHM breathing exercise. Can you influence on it?
  - **YES**
  - **NO** → Calm down, relax. Do yoga or fitness. Read a book. Watch TV. Do whatever makes you feel better.

Use the LHM F.T.S.A.L. Algorithm

Believe that everything has a reason why it happened. Believe in the best.

Exercise: For every step of the ***LHM PEACEFULLNESS FORMULA***, make your own association drawings.

1. ....

2. ....

3. ....

4. ....

5. ....

6. . . . .

Exercise: Make your own association drawings for the
LHM PEACEFULLNESS ALGORITHM

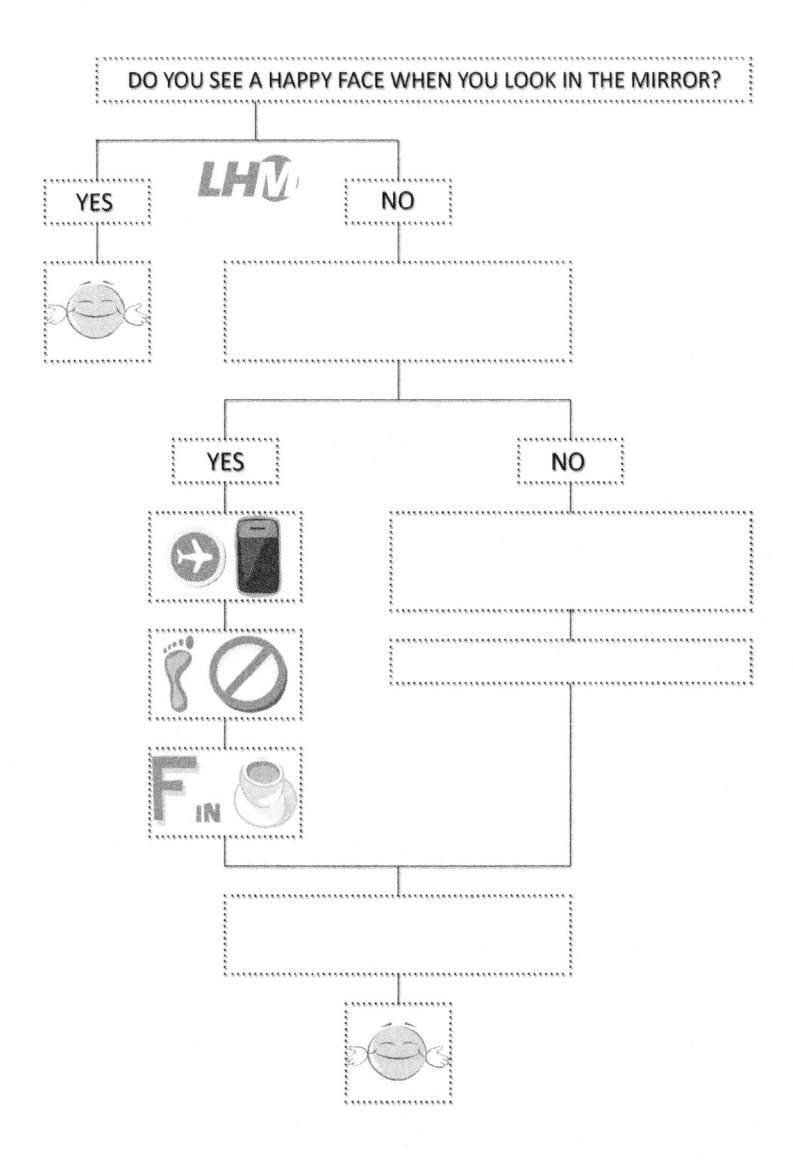

10. LHM IQ Training Question: What is the connection between hydrogen and oxygen, and fire and water?

. . . .

CHAPTER 11

AWAKENING

"Enlightened leadership is spiritual if we understand spirituality not as some kind of religious dogma or ideology but as the domain of awareness where we experience values like truth, goodness, beauty, love and compassion, and also intuition, creativity, insight and focused attention."

~ Deepak Chopra

I started to write this book for my own pleasure. For I love to write. First I wrote it as a blog. Some time had passed and I was doing a lot of meditation with Oprah and Deepak on their 21 days meditational challenges. And I started to get some answers from my inner voice that I had never heard via this practice before. At first, I ignored it, but it became louder and louder. When I thought about something and asked questions in my mind, during meditation I got answers and like a puzzle the pieces began to fall into place.

Suddenly, I possessed information I knew I had to spread and share with the rest of the world. And this I would do so everyone could benefit and understand. I also got the chance to learn about association memory and the connection between heart and mind. And that was it! My book took on another dimension and then became illustrated with descriptive images. These are my own unique associations, and provided in order to make the content more palatable and entertaining for everyone.

During this period of time, every day I would obtain newer and newer information. It included new books and new articles throughout the Internet that supported and validated my way of thinking, and which helped to "find their way to me." New people who were in this professional field also started to emerge and came to support me.

Then the obstacles I had in my life I began to solve, utilizing the LHM techniques I had developed as a first version. But at first, the techniques were complicated and difficult to implement. And in one meditation all I did was complain about it. Naturally, nothing happened. Then I complained again and again and again. Still nothing happened. Then I stopped complaining, and instead asked: "Please, I need help. The LHM techniques are complicated and no one will understand me."

Then a few days later I got the idea to create the LHM formulas and LHM algorithms that would help to develop a new kind of behavior designed to bring new and excellent results in people's lives. Then I decided to create the LHM IQ training questions in order to expand people's minds as well as their hearts. Eventually the book became more than just a book. It became a tool for heart and mind development, for emotional and intellectual development; and it became a workbook as well as a most valuable resource for bringing goodness and inner peace into my entire life.

Believe me, any time when I felt bad or was experiencing a difficult situation in my life, I would read this book I had created. I would draw. I would solve IQ questions or create new ones. For I didn't like the life I was living. I was very unhappy. And knew I had to try something revolutionary and would bring about great positive change. So, after this process of discovery and implementation, I became like a completely different person--a person who is now happy, satisfied, successful and loved. And when I make mistakes or encounter difficult situations today, I find the solution here, from this book. And every time I am surprised—and yet not so surprised—how it works! It feels almost like "someone" continues to test all of this on me. But I feel better! I feel good! I feel calm! And that is the only way to go! So test it on me as much as you like, whoever you are. I consider you my divine source. So what the heck, bring it on!

For our higher source--the God, the Universe or whoever or whatever you wish to call this amazing force--wants us here. This is obvious. And it wants to embrace us, nurture our souls and bring us good. But we made it difficult to live on Earth, so it is giving us a solution that can raise our awareness and make us feel as we should feel. And that is to feel fabulous and like the most perfect creatures on Earth. For my main intention is to bring good to this world, good to all people, so I am sharing everything that I know in this moment. And I will share more in future writings, as well.

Even now when I am writing this last chapter, I have all the words that I should say to you and I am not making them up by myself! The divine Universe gave them to me and my job is to share it with as many people I possibly can.

You started this flight with me…back at Chapter One. You are completing it with your soul now made more aware, to share with all the other souls who have earned a higher level of awareness. So welcome among us awakened people and invite everyone you love to experience Live from Your Heart and Mind! Let us share love and happiness together.

BE HAPPY, LIVE, LOVE AND LET IT BE

IQ TRAINING SOLUTIONS

Here are the solutions and answers to the LHM IQ training questions. Solutions are much more important than answers. They indicate the way of thinking which lead to an answer. When you learn this way of thinking, there is a higher chance that you will never forget these facts. And you can use this method as well as the association drawing method whenever you must learn something. This way you will activate your brain capacity on a higher level and it will help you in your professional and private life. Because if you learn to train your brain and develop its speed and associative thinking, you will be better in every situation, and with learning, problem solving, organizing and time management. And if you use all of it while standing on healthy emotional ground (developed with the LHM formulas and LHM algorithms), there will be no limit for you!

Some of these questions are fun, some are hiding scientific or interesting facts. Of course, we can discuss each one of them as my friends did with me, since they didn't know important facts and could not solve the questions at first. But the aim of these questions isn't to test your knowledge. The goal is for you to "get out of the box" and find new ways of thinking and activate your brain so that it can grow and develop further. But remember to have fun! Enjoy! And play this game with your friends. You can also make up your own questions. And make easier questions for your children. Until the age of three, children have almost 100% of their brain activated. Then, as they grow, if their brain is not trained, that % goes down until they become grownups.

1. LHM IQ training question:

What is common to a snowflake, cow and forefinger?

Solution:

1.1 What is the most famous fact about any snowflake?

It is unique.

1.2 And what do you have on your forefinger?

A fingerprint.

1.3 And what is the most famous fact about fingerprint?

It is unique.

1.4 So, what is unique to a cow?

It is a scientific fact that there is no cow with the same spots.

Answer to LHM IQ training question:

It is uniqueness. There are no two same snowflakes. There are no two same fingerprints. There are no two cows with the same spots.

2. LHM IQ training question:

What is common to the water in Australia and the planet Venus?

Solution:

2.1 What is specific for water in Australia?

It flows in a reverse direction compared to other continents.

2.2 What is specific to planet Venus?

Venus rotates in a reverse direction in relation to other planets.

Answer to LHM IQ training question:

It is reverse direction. Water turns in a reverse direction in Australia compared to other continents. Venus rotates in a reverse direction in relation to other planets.

3. LHM IQ training question:

If we suppose that all creatures on Earth can think and make decisions, what creature thinks from its head, even when it makes decisions from the heart?

Solution:

3.1 If you pay attention on the question form, you will notice that that creature is probably animal and that it thinks from its head which is usual, because the brain is in its head. But this animal makes heartfelt decisions from its head, too! What this could mean?

There is an animal which has a brain and heart in its head.

3.2 What animal has a brain and heart in its head?

It is the shrimp.

Aswer to LHM IQ training question:

It is the shrimp. A shrimp's brain and heart are in its head.

4. LHM IQ training question:

What is common to the Guinness Book of World Records and actress Sophie Nélisse?

Solution:

4.1. Do you know movies in which Sophie Nélisse acted?

If you do know, list them.

If you don't know, Google her and list them.

4.2 What is the Guinness Book of Records?

It is a book.

4.3 Is there any movie that you listed that has the word "book" in its title?

The Book Thief.

4.4 And what does the word "thief" have to do with the Guinness Book of Records?

The Guinness Book of Records is the most commonly stolen book from bookstores throughout the world.

Answer to LHM IQ training question:

It is the thievery. Sophie has starred in the movie, The Book Thief. The Guinness Book of Records is the most commonly stolen book from bookstores throughout the world.

5. LHM IQ training question:

What is the connection between Nikola Tesla and a dentist?

Solution:

5.1 What was the most important scientific field that Nikola Tesla worked on?

Electricity.

5.2. Where do you sit when you go to dentist?

You sit in a dentist chair.

5.3 And why is that chair different than other chairs?

It uses electricity.

5.4. Who was Nikola Tesla?

He was a scientist and inventor.

5.5 And what is the most important thing that he invented?

He invented alternating current electricity that powers the modern world.

5.6 And what was invented by a dentist? (Try to draw a conclusion based on previous answers: electricity and chair.)

The electric chair which is used for a death penalty was invented by a dentist.

Answer to LHM IQ training question:

It is electricity. Tesla invented alternating current electricity that powers the modern world. A dentist invented the electric chair which is used for a death penalty.

6. LHM IQ training question:

What is common to a duck and silence?

> **Solution:**
>
> 6.1 What is the only animal who does not create an echo when it produces a sound?
>
> *It is the duck. No one knows why.*
>
> 6.2 Does the silence have an echo?
>
> *No.*

Answer to LHM IQ training question:

A duck's quack does not echo. No one knows why. Silence also doesn't echo.

7. LHM IQ training question:

What connects the numbers 111.111.111 and 12.345.678.987.654.321?

> **Solution:**
>
> 7.1 What can you do to these numbers?
>
> *Read them.*

Look at them as a list and try to find some hidden solution.

Use - + / x on them.

Reverse them.

Answer to LHM IQ training question:

111.111.111 X 111.111.111 = 12.345.678.987.654.321.

8. LHM IQ training question:

What is common to elephants and plants?

Solution:

8.1 Have you ever seen an elephant that can jump?

No.

8.2 Can plants jump?

No.

Answer to LHM IQ training question:

Elephants are the only animals that cannot jump. Plants also cannot jump.

9. LHM IQ training question:

What is common to writers Miguel de Cervantes and William Shakespeare?

Solution:

9.1 Do you know the dates of their birth?

09/29/1547

04/26/1564

9.2 Do you know the date of their death?

04/23/1616

04/23/1616

Answer to LHM IQ training question:

They were the greatest writers in their countries, and they both died on the same day: 04/23/1616.

10. LHM IQ training question:

What is the connection between the hydrogen and oxygen, and fire and water?

Solution:

10.1 What is hydrogen?

It is a gas.

10.2 Is it flammable?

Yes it is.

10.3. What is oxygen?

It is a gas.

10.4. Can fire spread in an oxygen environment?

Yes. Oxygen enables combustion.

10.5 And what do hydrogen and oxygen make?

They make water.

10.6 And what does water do to the fire?

Water extinguishes fire.

Answer to LHM IQ training question:

Hydrogen is a flammable gas. Oxygen enables combustion. Combined they make water, which is used to extinguish fire.

THANK YOU

I need to give a personal thank you to all these wonderful people!

- My husband – I don't have words to describe him. He stayed with me in every situation, for 15 years now. He loves me and supports me. He is the biggest source of positive energy that I know in a person, and I will respect and love him until I die.

- My mother – She gave me unforgettable support and love, which made me a better person. She stood by me during every experience and gave me the strength to move on. It is enough for me to look at her and to see a great lifetime fighter who always made the impossible possible.

- My deceased grandparents - They were my teachers. They were my leaders and my idols when I was a little girl. They showed me how to respect, to love and to be kind and grateful.

- My family and friends – I love you more than anything in this world!

- Bryant McGill and Jenni Young – Incredibly unique people who have done and do so much as positive world changers. They are the guiding force behind Simple Reminders, SRN, The Royal Society, Thought Leader School, Peace Prize, and so much else. They are also high-level social media influencers reaching a billion people a year. And I am so happy and proud to be a part of their journey and contribute to changing the world to be a much more beautiful place. They have given me tremendous strength and support, and a lot of love and happiness. And I believe they give the same to the whole world. Thank you so much, Bryant and Jenni!

I also would like to mention all the members of The Royal Society who are such amazing and supportive people! Each of us shares support, love, motivation, knowledge, happiness and inspiration openly and with grace. Thank you, one and all!

- Kriz Armytage – Wonderful lady from Australia who supported me all the way. Maybe she didn't know that, but she was my strength when I started this LHM story. She is admin of the FB page "Hunting Happiness Project," and via her every post and comment to my posts and sites she raised me up and made me believe that there is a reason to do all this. Thank you, Kriz!

- The Wellness Universe – Is a wonderful community of positive world changers! The WU has given me a ton of love, support, and strength, and brought a lot of happiness, soul power and positive energy to me and I believe to the whole world. Its founders and all members are so amazing and supportive! Each one of us in his and her own way shares love, happiness, inspiration, motivation and knowledge with the whole world. Thanks to the entire WU!

- Oprah – I don't have words to describe her. If I want anything in my life, I would love to see her in person, hug her and tell her "Thank you, Oprah, for everything you have given to this world!"

- Rhonda Byrne – As I said earlier in this book, I don't know if I would be alive if it wasn't for her. Thank you, Rhonda. Thank you, thank you, thank you for writing "The Secret" and showing it to the world!

- Robin Sharma – This man changed my way of thinking. He changed my life! Thank you, Robin, for the "Leader without a title" philosophy. It completely turned over my existence to the better way!

- Iyanla Vanzant – She is so divine! I adore her voice and her existence. I feel that everything she talks about is from a higher source and that she is one of the most aware people in the world who will continue to change so many lives! Thank you, Iyanla, for being as you are!

- Louise L Hay – As one of the pioneers of positive psychology and positive affirmations, this lady already has changed millions and millions lives as she has changed mine. Thank you, Louise, for the crucial foundation and for starting a positive wave in my life!

- Joe Vitlae – From the very first, he introduced me to the thought that we are creating everything in our life, even if it is something bad like a car accident. Thank you, Joe, for being so direct and for pointing this out in such a cosmic way!

- Brian Tracy – I think that everybody knows who he is. He has a completely different look at life and provides a lot of practical techniques which have changed millions of lives. Some things become so much easier with his philosophy. Thank you, Brian!

- Jack Canfield – Jack your soup has been more than a cure for my soul! Thank you!

- Bob Proctor – Big thanks to one of the most powerful speakers who has changed millions upon millions of lives around planet Earth. Because of him I also want to kiss my own hand. Thank you, Bob!

- Paolo Coelho – He is more than a great soul. He is a great person. I grew up with his novel The Alchemist, and he was the first one who introduced me to my inner self. When my country was suffering from huge floods, I wrote to him and he recorded a video to give his support and invited other people to help us. Thank you, Paolo!

- Anthony De Mello – Anthony, I woke up because of you! Thank you so much!

- Dalai Lama – If there is a modern saint it is the Dalai Lama. Thank you for all the good that you give to humanity! My respect and thank you!

- Steve Jobs – Steve showed me what really matters. And I recognized absolute truth: We all will die, anyway. So live life, make it wonderful and let others live theirs. RIP and thank you, Steve.

- Bill Gates – Bill showed his great heart after he left Microsoft. I became positively surprised with his current work. He is the one of the greatest persons on Earth and I just want to say Thank you, Bill, for everything that you did in IT. But much more thanks for what are you doing now. Great minds do great things!

- Robert Kiyosaki – So smart, so great, so helpful! Robert is one of the people who inspired me to take things in my own hands and make it happen. Thank you, Robert!

- Deepak Chopra – He healed my soul. With his meditations on Oprah's network, I got up every time I fell down. Every obstacle was defeated in an alpha state of mind during his meditations. And, as the frosting on the cake, at the end of the creative process of my writing this book, many answers came to me during these meditations. Thank you, Deepak!

- Beyoncé – I had the operation, and from bed my husband took me to her concert because he knew that I would feel better. And I did come to feel better. Thank you, Beyoncé, for your energy, for your positive attitude, for your existence!

- ZAZ – I wanted so much to see her because she is complete positive energy and she came to my city when no one expected! I was in the first row and that was the battery charge concert. So, thank you, Zaz. Thank you for coming to the public and for giving all that great frequency to all of us!

Now you saw who are the authors that changed my life as well as people who inspired me. I am, also, very grateful to a lot more people who came in and out of my life. While I was writing this book I met so many wonderful people, and one book would not be enough to mention them all. I am grateful that I had chance to meet such wonderful people and I will make sure that they know it!

By reading this book, my dear reader, you also came into my life, and I am grateful to you. And you should be grateful to yourself because you allowed yourself to open this new door. Let the LHM formulas, LHM algorithms and LHM IQ training became part of your life and make your life extraordinary. And I will be more than happy if we made it happen together! I wish you a wonderful life filled with love and happiness.

With Love,

Catherine B. Roy

ABOUT THE AUTHOR

Catherine B. Roy is a bestselling author, Heart and Mind Coach, Human Potential Thought Leader and award-winning artist and scientist whose stimulating, upbeat and inspirational writings have helped countless people in the world. It has helped them solve problems, infuse their lives with hope, energy and success, and remarkably improve people's personal and professional relationships.

She enjoyed the distinction of receiving the 30 Under 30 Young Leaders award and is also an experienced linguistics researcher, with published scientific works in the fields of pragmatism, communication and psycho-linguistics.

As the Thought Leader on SRN.net and author of published articles on The Huffington Post, The Simple Reminders, The Wellness Universe, The Spirituality Post, Guided Mind and several published books, Catherine's approach to life, growth and all living things is one infused with positive faith, knowledge and conviction.

As the author and founder of the "Live from Your Heart and Mind" (LHM) community, Catherine is the guiding force behind the LHM system for increasing a person's emotional and intellectual capacity, and inspiring them to positive change and accomplishment.

One of the most important and beautiful things that separates LHM from other systems is the fact that LHM algorithms are created as a personal guide. There are no two same persons on this planet, and there will be no same solution. LHM solutions are created to be suitable for anyone in a wide variety of situations and based on individual answers. LHM's greater mission is achieving a balanced, happy and successful life for everyone who uses it.

LHM

Printed in Great Britain
by Amazon